While studying to become a teacher, **Diana Beaver** realized that, unless students were in learning mode, 'teaching' simply wasted everybody's time; so she gave up teaching and began to study learning instead.

In the course of this study, she read *Frogs into Princes* by Richard Bandler and John Grinder, which proved to her entire satisfaction that things she had always known (and which you have always known) were true; for example: we are all different, and we all do things differently; and, if we are not feeling our best, we will not produce our best. This was Neuro-Linguistic Programming; it made complete sense, and she realized that it would revolutionize her work. Since then she has been lucky enough to work with most of NLP's finest trainers around the world.

She works in learning, business, health, sport, the law, and any other area that grabs her interest – both training and one-to-one.

Diana lives in the Cotswolds, England, with her husband; they have two grown up sons, a dog and a cat.

nlp

for lazy learning
how to learn faster and more effectively

diana beaver

vega

ISBN 1-84333-049-0

A catalogue record for this book is available from the British
Library

first published in 2002 by
Vega
64 Brewery Road
London, N7 9NT

A member of the Chrysalis Group plc

Visit our website at www.chrysalisbooks.co.uk

Printed in Great Britain by CPD, Wales

Contents

Acknowledgements   vii

Introduction   ix

About Learning   1

About Not Learning   30

Pause for Thought: What Do You Want?   56

Come to Your Senses!   60

Pause for Thought: How Will You Know?   94

Some Tricks of the Trade   97

Pause for Thought: About our 'Elders and Betters'   126

Mentors, Metaphors and Models   128

    David Edwards   137

    Catherine Harman   141

    Adam Palmer   144

    Lucinda Green MBE   151

    Colin Reeve   158

    Sir John Harvey-Jones MBE   164

    Terence Stamp   169

    Judith DeLozier   176

A Message from Dr Richard Bandler   184

Bibliography   185

Some Useful Addresses   190

Index   192

DEDICATION

This book is dedicated, with my love and thanks, to my friend, teacher and mentor Dr John Grinder.

It is also for my menfolk, Philip, Mark and Hugo, who, despite suffering almost total neglect, have been endlessly supportive; with special thanks to my husband, Philip, for the countless hours he has spent on the computer creating programs for me, speeding things up and doing everything else he could think of to make my work easier.

Acknowledgements

I should like to thank all the friends and colleagues who have given me permission to plunder their work. I hope that I have given credit where credit is due for everything that I have taken from other people and, if I have not, that the creators will forgive me.

My thanks also to the trainers, mentors and friends that I have been lucky enough to work with: Richard Bandler, Charlotte Bretto, Judith DeLozier, Robert Dilts, Todd Epstein, Lara Ewing, David Gaster, Stephen Gilligan, John Grinder, Ian McDermott, Joseph O'Connor, Julian Russell, Titos Sompa, and especially to Judy, John, Robert, Todd and Stephen, from whom I have had so much wisdom, and with whom I have had so much fun. It was when working with the late David Gaster that I had one of my best glimpses of the blinding obvious: *in order to go farther than we ever dreamed was possible, all we need to do is to let go.*

I am particularly grateful to my models of excellence, who have so generously given me their time and so patiently and good-humouredly answered my endless questions: Judith DeLozier, David Edwards, Lucinda Green MBE, the late Catherine Harman, Sir John Harvey-Jones MBE, Adam Palmer, Colin Reeve and Terence Stamp. My thanks too, to all my colleagues, students and clients, from whom I have learned so much.

Le Lieutenant-Colonel (e.r.) Georges Margot, *Ecuyer en Chef* of the Cadre Noir from 1946 to 1956, has kindly given permission to use the illustration on page 157 in memory of his wife Janine, who really knew what friendship was.

I would like to thank Robert Dilts and Todd Epstein of the Dynamic Learning Center for their kind permission to use their copyrighted material: the logical levels diagram and the Jungle Gym; Routledge & Kegan Paul for permission to reproduce the diagrams showing how we read and the triune brain from *The Brain Book* by Peter Russell; John Harvey-Jones for permission to quote from '*Making it Happen*'; Spike Milligan and Penguin Books for permission to quote '*Free Flight*' and David Lewis and the Souvenir Press for permission to use the illustration from *Mind Skills* on page 63.

Introduction

Have you ever thought that you could not learn something? Have you ever found that your brain closed down when you were under stress? Do you have difficulty in solving problems? Has your communication ever been misunderstood? Do you ever allow yourself to be bullied? Do you have a horror of speaking in public? Do you believe that you will fail unless you give yourself a hard time? Do you procrastinate when faced with a difficult situation? Do you ever feel inadequate? Do you want to enjoy life more?

If your answer to any of these questions is 'yes', then this book will change your thinking about yourself.

For as long as I can remember, I have worked with people – adults as well as children – who were having difficulty with learning; and I could never understand why they were not doing well because they were all so bright.

We are all natural-born Superlearners. The only problem with your mind is that you were born without a handbook. *NLP for Lazy Learning* fills that gap by helping you to discover how you operate your learning equipment, and how to enhance the learning channels that you were born with but may have forgotten how to use.

In the late 80s, I was a student on a weekend teacher training course which went completely to pieces; staff and students argued furiously and I went home confused and bewildered by everyone's behaviour, including my own. Then I had a glimpse of the blinding obvious: people can teach for all they are worth and yet if the students are not in 'learning mode', everyone is wasting their time. So I gave up teaching and turned my attention to learning.

Then I came across the concept of Neuro-Linguistic Programming™ otherwise known as NLP. Although the name is enough to glaze the eyes of any polite enquirer, the concept is unbelievably simple: it applies objectivity (which is the way we are supposed to think) to subjectivity (which is the way we really think, because we are humans, rather than robot). It made complete sense and I realized at once that this would revolutionize my work. NLP began in the early 70s as a twinkle in the eye of a mathematician and computer wizard called Richard Bandler who was interested in therapy. While he was a student at the University of California in Santa Cruz, he joined forces with John Grinder, Professor of Linguistics at the UC, and the two of them worked together to put NLP on the map.

NLP has been described as the study of the structure of subjective experience: how the way we process our thoughts affects our internal experience; how our internal experience affects our behaviour; and how our behaviour affects everyone else. NLP is a way of thinking about thinking. It is about how we know things. How do you know that you like spending time with one person rather than with another? How do you know that you cannot learn something? How do you know that you want to read this book? What process inside you gives you your information?

The name, Neuro-Linguistic Programming, describes the components of this combination of art and techniques.

Neuro: information is stored in our nervous system, which reacts in one way or another to every situation, for example, scientists have measured over 1,500 different neurological responses to stress.

Linguistic: the language that we use demonstrates, at a deep subconscious level, what is going on inside us; for example, if I ask you to look at something from my point of view, I am processing my thoughts in pictures, and inviting you to do the same; if you reply that we are getting bogged down with detail, I will realize that you are not into pictures at the moment – you are processing through your feelings, and your feelings are that we are not getting anywhere very fast.

Programming: in order to save time and effort in checking out each piece of information that we receive, we run automatic programmes, for example, we see a red light and we stop, without thinking; someone smiles at us, and we smile back. Some of us run programmes that are out of date: we may panic when we see a spider, or are asked to take a test or make a speech, or if someone mentions mathematics; we may die a thousand deaths if we make a mistake, or if somebody laughs at us. And one of the questions that NLP asks is: are these programmes still useful, or would we rather have choices in how we react?

NLP is the study of excellence: what is the difference that makes the difference between someone who does something with ease, elegance and excellence, and someone who does not?

This book gives you the chance to rediscover all those import ant things that you have always known at a very deep level, but which may have been considered frivolous or stupid by your 'elders and betters'. It is a study of the natural process of learning, and how and why we do it; it is also a study of the much more difficult process of 'not learning' and how and why we manage to do that. It is a book about you and how you operate: how your brain affects your body and how your body affects your brain. It is not a collection of hard facts about other people; if you want hard facts, you will find plenty to get your teeth into in the bibliography.

I would like to invite you to suspend your beliefs about learning and play around with mine for a while. And, when you have finished the book, you can keep everything that is or may be useful to you, and discard the rest.

Freedom

A bird in flight,
   her wings spread wide,
Is the soul of man
   with bonds untied.
Beyond the plough,
   the spade, the hod
A bird flies in
   the face of God.
Yet I with reason
   bright as day,
Forever tread
   the earthbound clay.

Spike Milligan

About Learning

In my experience, it is extremely difficult to teach grown-up people anything. It is, however, relatively easy to create conditions under which people will teach themselves.

Sir John Harvey-Jones, *Making it Happen*

We are all born learners. Between birth and the age of three we discover, among a million other things, how to master the extraordinarily complicated processes of sitting up, standing, walking, talking, feeding ourselves, creating relationships with other people, getting them to do what we want, playing ... and no one teaches us any of this; we learn it all for ourselves. For this reason I find it difficult to believe that we have anything other than extraordinary learning powers, and I wonder what would happen if you suspended for the moment any beliefs you may have to the contrary and just allowed yourself to read my thoughts, play the games, try the experiments and have fun. As *NLP for Lazy Learning* is based on the premise that we are all different, let us start with who we are and what we have in common.

WHO WE ARE

We are members of the human race and as such we are imbued with some of the curious quirks of human nature. The one that fascinates me most is our tendency to feel inadequate. I have a theory that most of us feel less than adequate quite a lot of the time: we walk into a room full of people and somehow become aware that A is better dressed than we are, B is more laid back than we are, C is more intelligent than we are, and so on. And we probably believe that we are the only inadequate person in the room because we imagine that everybody else feels perfectly OK.

We are survivors. Unlike the chick who climbs out of its egg and can race around and feed itself on day one, we rely on others to look after us for a comparatively long time. At a very early age we learn to communicate our wishes to those who see to our well-being. We also learn that in order to guarantee our physical and mental comfort it is a good plan to please those people.

We are natural-born learners – we have to be because we need to know about our environment in order to survive. Our world has so much information that we cannot retain it all inside our heads. In order to simplify things, we learn to create our own internal representations of reality through our five senses. We code and store information via internal pictures and sounds, feelings, tastes and smells. However we have chosen to do this, we also need to be aware that our coding system is not reality; it is simply our personal representation of reality. We only have to read or hear different eyewitness accounts of the same event to be aware of what reality is not.

In order to file all our knowledge efficiently in our heads, we learn to sort and label. This ability has evolved into the modern passion for labelling people and wanting to put them into boxes; in order to be allowed into the 'right' box, we are expected to conform, to be normal, to be like everybody else, otherwise we might end up in the 'wrong' box, which would reflect badly on people who are close to us.

We are trial-and-error learners. The only problem with the brain is that we are born without a handbook, so we have to work out how to use it as we go along. Some of us hit upon superb learning strategies (probably quite by chance), while some of us discover less efficient strategies, which we continue to use because we are unaware that there are other options available. Who taught you to walk? Did a professional adult teach you exactly which muscles to use or did you discover walking for yourself? Who taught you to speak? Did you have to learn to conjugate regular verbs before you were allowed to talk or did you simply copy the sounds made by the people around you until you got a reaction that told you that you had made sense?

We are creative learners. In our search for knowledge we are constantly trying out new things to see what will happen. While a grown-up is busy cooking we are busy exploring the lower half of the kitchen, where we may discover that banging saucepan lids together makes a satisfactory noise, that a saucepan is a perfect container for detergent, that dog food spreads nicely on the door or that we can make patterns in the detergent that we spilt on the floor – and this sort of creativity is discouraged because it makes a mess or a noise. A cardboard box can become a train, a boat, a car; a sheet can become a den, a cloak, a disguise; and we can become whoever we want to be. We are also creative with language, experimenting with sounds until we are understood, and gradually constructing whole, original sentences to express our unique, original ideas.

Our imagination is boundless but as we get older our parents are convinced that it is important for us to live in the real world, so as time goes by we are discouraged from seeing things that are not there ('Don't be silly, there are no such things as dragons'), from telling stories ('How many times do I have to tell you? Mrs Black is not a witch'), from making things up ('That is not true ... and you know what happens to children who tell lies'). To make matters worse, modern education concentrates on so-called academic subjects, these are what intelligent children do, so art, craft, and music may be considered a waste of time.

We are unique, like our fingerprints. There is no one else exactly like you in the whole world, and this makes you very special. If we both think about a dog, your thoughts will not be the same as mine. We will not be seeing the same pictures in our mind's eye, we will not be hearing the same sounds in our mind's ear and we will not be experiencing the same feelings. If I ask you to think about a dog galloping towards you, and you have recently had an unpleasant encounter with a rottweiler, your internal experience will not be the same as mine, as I think about our beloved flatcoat rushing up to welcome me home.

What goes on inside us affects not only our behaviour, but also other people's behaviour towards us; and often we are not consciously aware of what is going on inside us.

NLP-ers are modellers. This is our technical term for discovering what is going on inside other people, what the structure of their subjective experience is. How do they do whatever it is that they are doing? How does A do mental arithmetic at such speed? What processes go on inside him to achieve an answer to a numbers problem that makes us go pale just thinking about it? How does B communicate so effectively? What is she doing with her brain and body in order to know which questions to ask? And how does she remember the answers? What is it about C's beliefs system that allows him to take to any new foreign language like a duck to water? How does D remember her bank account number, her credit card number and the dates of everybody's birthdays? We may not want or need to be able to do any of these things ourselves, but you never know when the structure of these strategies might come in useful for something else we may want to do.

Another aspect of modelling is to help us to discover how people sabotage themselves. How has A convinced himself that the world is out to get him, while the rest of us believe that he has everything going for him? What is going on inside him that convinces him that everyone is his sworn enemy? Does he see doom-and-gloom pictures in his mind's eye? Does he have insidious voices in his mind's ear? Does he have a feeling that frightens him?

We are all born with the same sort of learning equipment, and we all have different strategies for making use of this equipment. Modelling helps us to expand our own models of the world, to provide us with new ideas and strategies to play with, and to give us choices in how we are going to react in specific situations. What would happen to our communication skills if we took on the belief that every single person that we met was utterly fascinating? What would happen to our language skills if we found ourselves surrounded by delightful, interesting and interested people and not an interpreter in sight?

Here is an experiment devised by Judith DeLozier, who is an international NLP trainer. You will need to find someone to do it with (preferably someone not at all like you), and half an hour to spare. Once you have done it and discovered how fascinating it is, you will then want to try it with lots more people.

> One of you is going to go for a walk for ten minutes. You can go anywhere you like and do anything you want; this is your ten minutes. You are the model. The other one is going to follow the model, and copy *everything* that person does: the way they walk, the way they hold their head; the way they swing their arms, their rhythm, everything. The follower, or modeller, is going to 'become' the person in front for those ten minutes. This is about seeing and feeling: conversation is not allowed until the ten minutes are up, when the modeller can tell the model what he or she experienced. Then reverse roles and try it again.

This is an experiment to stretch your mind: by changing your physiology – the way you hold yourself and move – you will discover just how differently each of us experiences the world according to the models that we have created inside our head. You will discover where different people place their attention, and what difference those changes make to you and the way you think and feel. Try them on for size and ask yourself when those changes might be useful for you: when you could borrow the other person's physiology to help you to think in a different way.

We are all part of a system. At home, with our families, we are part of the family system; at work we are part of the work system; in a learning environment we are part of that system. What goes on in that system affects us. For example, if there is a disagreement in the family, we are going to be affected either by being directly involved or by the imbalance in the system that has been created by the disagreement. In the same way, if we come home in a bad temper, the rest of the family system is going to be affected by us: they may try to avoid us; they may try to jolly us out of it; they may respond by matching our behaviour, consciously or unconsciously.

WHY WE LEARN

We learn because we are born with insatiable curiosity about the world in which we live. We want to know, so we find out and, because we wanted to know, we remember. When we are small everything that we achieve is reinforced by cries of joy and admiration from doting members of our family, who probably think we are the most advanced infant in the world: we believe in ourselves, because no one has told us any different.

As we get bigger, things change as people begin to tell us that we are not perfect, thinking it is for our own good. This does not affect our inborn curiosity and need to explore, and the fact that we do not necessarily want to learn what other people think we ought to know does not mean that we cannot learn. For example, think about something you really like doing, and then allow yourself to become aware of just how much you have learned about whatever it is, probably without having made the slightest effort. When you are having fun, learning just happens without your noticing it. Jean's father was a mathematician and used to beat her when she could not understand arithmetic, so anything to do with maths is impossible as far as she is concerned. Jean is a professional embroiderer, using algebra to calculate how much material she needs, geometry to design and arithmetic to work out how much it is going to cost. Fortunately, no one has ever told her that this is mathematics; she believes that it is all to do with embroidery, so she finds it perfectly simple.

Our beliefs get formed in interesting ways: 'Cats keep elephants out of the garden': I know that this is true, because we have cats and we never suffer from elephants in the garden. We all make mistakes, and *a mistake is no big deal: it is simply part of the learning process.*

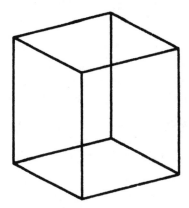

The Necker Cube

Look at the drawing of the cube. Is it on the floor or on the ceiling? If you look at it for long enough, with relaxed eyes, you will find that the cube appears to move. This is because your brain needs to make sense of things and it has no exterior reference point here, so it will go on trying different ideas until it can find something that does make sense. From the moment we are born we are discovering strategies that work, and then testing them. The child who drops something from its high-chair for the tenth time, and screams with rage when an exasperated lackey refuses to pick it up yet again, is testing its recently discovered theory about gravity. Once a theory is considered properly tested and proved, it goes into the data bank as a fact, because we believe it to be so.

As you discovered when reading my beliefs about cats and elephants, things that are stored in our belief systems do not necessarily have anything to do with reality; and if as a child we have been endlessly told by our 'elders and betters' that we are stupid, we are likely to believe it, because they supposedly know better, and therefore must be right. And if we believe that we cannot learn, we will not be able to learn. Try this experiment.

Think about something that you believe in and then think of something that you do not believe in. Then switch from one thought to the other and compare what is going on inside you as you think about each one. For example:

- Do you see pictures in your mind's eye? Where are those different pictures? Are they in colour or black-and-white? Are they still or moving pictures? Which is the bigger picture? Which is the closer picture?

- Do you hear any sounds in your mind's ear? Which sounds are the louder? Which sounds are the closer? Are they voices? If so, whose voices are they?

- What feelings do you have about each thought? Where do you experience those feelings?

- What else do you notice about your body – its temperature, lightness, size, and so on?

- What is happening inside your head?

There will be a whole range of different responses because you have one internal file for 'believe' and one for 'disbelieve'; this is part of the way you have refined the workings of your brain so that you can check things out quickly. What we believe in and value contributes to our sense of identity. If we feel that someone is attacking our beliefs, it could be a threat to our identity. In order to protect ourselves, we may hang on to our beliefs at all costs, refusing to admit any possibility of doubt. Have you ever been greeted with less than enthusiasm when you have tried to introduce a new idea or discovery? The reaction was nothing personal; you had simply upset someone's belief system and wobbled the foundation on which a fragile identity was based.

Many of us were brought up with the curious belief 'No pain, no gain', or, to put it another way, 'it's too easy, therefore it cannot work'. I wonder why we are so determined to give ourselves a hard time.

When I first met Rebecca, she was having terrible head-aches from the stress she was creating for herself at school, because she had filed the question of her intelligence with the things that she did not believe. Once she had moved it into her 'believe' file, everything changed and she was able to get on with what she was born to do.

She spent the whole school year having fun – until the day before her exams started, when her belief in her own intelligence began to wobble. She telephoned me to say that her friends had been studying until three and four in the morning while she had not done anything that she considered to be work for a whole year; what was going to happen if she had made a mistake and got it all wrong? We spent some time together restoring her lazy learning state. She took exams in nine subjects, and got nine As.

It is we who programme our brains in the first place. They are our brains, and there to work for us; they will do exactly as they are asked.

HOW WE LEARN

Different ways of representing our world – the five senses

Some of us learn best through our eyes: we see internal pictures, which may be concrete or abstract. All good spellers *see* the word in their mind's eye, although they may not consciously be aware of this. If you ask people a question and they look up before answering, they are checking out the information in their store of internal pictures. 'Don't look up at the ceiling – the answer's not up there', we say impatiently, but the ceiling is probably exactly where the answer is for visual learners.

Some of us learn best through our ears. People who turn their best ear towards you while you are talking, instead of looking at you, are doing you the courtesy of giving you their fullest attention. When you ask them a question, auditory learners will look from side to side to check out internal sounds. 'Look at me when I'm talking to you!' we insist, immediately depriving auditory learners of their best system.

Some of us learn most through our bodies: we need to handle, play with or do whatever it is we are trying to learn about, so that our muscles can remember what it feels like. People who move around while you are talking to them are working the information into their muscles. 'Sit still! Stop fiddling!' we insist of kinaesthetic learners, paralysing their bodies and thus paralysing their minds. Kinaesthetic people will check out information via their feelings by looking down towards the hand they write with.

Taste becomes a less available way of learning as we grow older. Babies immediately put everything in their mouths as part of their research, but this is soon discouraged because of 'germs'; there was a blind diamond dealer who tested every stone by putting it in his mouth. Of course, well-behaved children do not go around smelling people and things, do they? I remember a stallholder in a vegetable market in Berlin telling me that I was not allowed to smell the tomatoes. When I replied that if I could not smell them, I would not buy them, she was astounded – this did not compute with her model of the world. Maybe it is because we cannot go around sniffing things too obviously in public that smell remains such a powerful unconscious emotional trigger.

Try an experiment.

You have won a holiday; which venue will you choose?

- A luxurious hotel, with all the creature comforts you can imagine; excellent indoor and outdoor sporting facilities; multigym, massage and sauna.

- Beautifully situated hotel, recently redecorated in excellent taste, with landscaped garden and splendid views; colour TV in every room and video service.

- Quiet hotel in peaceful surroundings, away from the endless clamour of daily life; wake in the morning to the sound of birdsong and the fountain playing in the courtyard.

- A gastronomic holiday in an hotel that prides itself on the quality of the food: everything is home-grown or reared to produce the finest dishes you could hope to enjoy anywhere.

So which would be the best hotel for you, and why?

This is a very simple illustration of how different we are. I described the same hotel in different ways to appeal to the different senses, and you chose the one you preferred. Good advertising represents what is being promoted by appealing to as many of the senses as possible. Now that you have discovered which system you favour most in order to represent the world, you can try the test on your friends.

Of course, we do not always stay in the same system, but most of us have one that we prefer. You can tell which system people are in by the words that they use.

- Now, look here!
- Listen!
- How do you feel about that?
- I smell a rat.
- It leaves a nasty taste in your mouth.

These are not just catch phrases; they are unconscious expressions of what is going on inside us. It is interesting to listen to the words and phrases that people use and to watch their eye movements. There are other clues: visual people talk fast, trying to keep up with the pictures that are flashing through their minds; auditory people talk at a medium pace – words are their medium; and kinaesthetic people are slower and calmer, while they check everything out with their feelings.

Learning is simply a process of taking in information through our five senses and filing it somewhere. To prove that we have learned it, we have to be able to find the file we put it in; and so as with all filing, a good cross-reference system is useful. The things that we remember best are those that engaged the most of our neurology – in other words, when we learned them, our whole nervous system was involved: we can still see the pictures, hear the sounds, feel the feelings, taste the tastes and smell the smells.

When Joseph O'Connor, an NLP Master practitioner, is teaching music, he asks his students what major and minor notes taste and smell like. It might sound crazy, but it works: his students can tell the difference between major and minor in next to no time.

Our brains

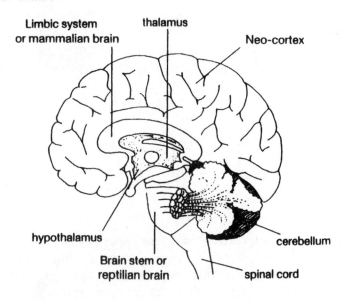

The Triune Brain

The reason why we say people have 'brains' is because we have more than one, and each is responsible for different things. The reptilian brain, or brain stem, is our oldest brain, and is responsible for our survival. It is your reptilian brain that, even though you were able to go to sleep with the radio or television on, wakes you up instantly at a sound that might mean that something is wrong. The mammalian brain, or limbic system, is the second oldest brain and looks after our emotions, and our fun.

The left and right brains form the two sides of the newest of our brains (the neo-cortex), which has made mankind the so-called masters of the world (although there are people who would argue that dolphins' brains are more evolved than ours). They are connected to each other by the *corpus callosum*, through which our thoughts can flow from one side to the other as freely as we allow them to do so. Each side of the new brain does a different job, and we need the input from both sides in order to be able to function at our best.

The left brain is a precise, ordered and methodical brain, which is responsible for language, calculation and organization. The right brain is an expansive, all-encompassing brain, which takes in the whole picture in a flash. To compare the different functions of your left and right brains, think about the picture of Robert Redford on page 13 *without turning back to it*. If you are saying to yourself that it was not a picture of Robert Redford you must prove it without turning back to it. Of course, what I am asking is ridiculous. But how did you know? I imagine that when I mentioned Robert Redford a picture of him came up in your mind's eye and you compared it to the other picture, also in your mind's eye, and knew at once that they were not the same person. This was a pretty amazing piece of computing, and it was all done in a flash by your right brain. In order to have proved that I was talking rubbish your left brain would have to have had two real pictures available, plus a ruler for precise measurements of each feature, and the process would have taken ages. A third option is that you might have felt stupid at not remembering the picture of Robert Redford, automatically assuming that I was right and you were wrong.

All these brains are connected to each other and to the rest of your body by the nervous system. A message from your new brain to your left big toe passes through your mammalian brain (emotions) and your reptilian brain (survival) on its way; and a message in the other direction, from your right thumb to your new brain, must also pass through the older brains, through your emotions and your survival instinct.

Brain waves

Our brains operate at different frequencies, depending upon what we are doing.

- *Delta waves* occur in deep, dreamless sleep.
- *Theta waves* are present between sleeping and waking, and in those moments when a brilliant idea comes to us although we seemed to be 'miles away'. These are the brainwaves of inspiration. Have you ever had a wonderful thought on waking and then lost it because you did not write it down?
- *Alpha waves* appear when we are relaxed enough to allow our thoughts to flow freely, and be creative,
- *Beta waves* are busy, bossy brain waves, which dominate when we are under pressure or being competitive.

Busy, bossy beta waves develop over the years. Babies, as you would expect, use mostly delta waves because they spend the majority of their time asleep. Between the ages of one and five theta waves dominate. At about five the alpha waves come in and gradually increase until we are using them as much as theta waves. In our teens alpha waves increase, theta waves decrease and beta waves start to appear; because they are so competitive, beta waves may well do their best to take over from alpha waves.

The problem with beta waves is that they are there at the expense of theta (inspiration) and alpha (free-flowing thought) waves. David Lewis, who wrote *The Alpha Plan*, has electric trains that he wires up to people's brains. The trains will only run on alpha waves. Imagine the scene: a group of competitive people about to have a train race, and because they want to win, they are in beta, so their trains will not budge. The object of this exercise is for people to retrain their brains to run on alpha waves, so that they can recapture the alert, relaxed state of childhood, when they learned so easily, simply absorbing knowledge like sponges. The wonderful thing about your brain is that it works for you and only for you, and it can do anything that you want.

Brain cells

We have 12,000–15,000 million brain cells each. There is a thought virus going round that, as we get older, some of our brain cells die, which means that we can no longer learn; and that we lose our memories. Even if we do lose some cells, it is useful to remember that a bee has only 9,000 to start with, and manages to lead an extraordinarily complicated life.

Thought creates connections between our brain cells; it creates pathways for further thought; and the more we use our brains, the more connections and paths we create; in other words, the more we learn, the easier it becomes to learn more.

> Once upon a time, when the land was covered in forest, a very small animal wanted to go from A to B, so it made its way through new, strange territory, leaving signs of its passage for the observant eyes of other creatures who followed it. As time went by, larger animals began to take the path, which became easier and easier to find the more it was used. Then people discovered that it was the best way to get from A to B. And the more the path was used, the easier it became to use it.
>
> Then the wheel was invented, and the path became even wider. Over time it changed and developed, and now we can get from A to B at enormous speed. And, because of all the other paths, which at one time did not exist, we can now go wherever we want, at whatever speed we choose.

The conscious and unconscious mind

I find it very difficult to separate brain and body; they are, after all, both part of the same system that is you. If I stick a pin into your finger, your brain is going to know about it; and if I wire your arm up to a lie detector and tell you that you will need to turn the page in a minute, the micro-muscle movement in your arm will register even though you are only thinking about turning the page. Instead of referring to brain and body as two different entities, therefore, I use the word 'mind' to encompass the whole system.

Timothy Gallwey, who developed *the Inner Game* to over-come the mental obstacles that prevent maximum performance in sport, created the concept of Self 1 and Self 2. Self 1 is the person who tells you *to try*, *to concentrate*, and warns you that you are about to *make a mistake*; whereas Self 2 knows how to do it and, left to its own devices, will produce the perfect result. Think of a time when you have played a brilliant shot or got yourself out of a tricky situation by doing something extraordinary, which you know you could not reproduce if you tried: that was Self 2 in action.

In his book *Superdriver*, John Whitmore, ex-racing driver and sports psychologist, encouraged me to allow my unconscious mind to do the driving. I tried it, tentatively. A flashy red car came around the corner on my side of the road and I reacted perfectly, getting myself out of trouble without even noticing that I was in it. From that moment I allowed my internal driver to take charge. Some time later I met John Whitmore and complained that I had been so relaxed one day that I had missed my turning, driven ten miles out of the way and arrived late. He roared with laughter and said, 'You didn't specify where you wanted to go, did you?' He was quite right; I had not. Now I get into my car, visualize my destination and then leave my unconscious mind to do the rest, which means that I arrive at the other end as fresh as a daisy.

Here is a puzzle that cannot be solved by logic, so you might like to give it to your unconscious mind, sleep on it and see what you dream about. What does this represent:

H I J K L M N O?

(The answer is on page 29)

Neuro-Linguistic Programmers believe that any behaviour, however extraordinary, has a positive intention: that it is our unconscious mind's way of getting something important for us. The person who is overweight may subconsciously believe that extra pounds provide extra protection; the person who cannot learn may think that life is safer at the bottom of the class, because there is no further to fall; the aggressive person may be protecting a frightened person inside. Whatever metaphor you choose for the two sides of our nature, be it left/right brains, beta/alpha brainwaves, Self 1/Self 2, or the conscious/unconscious minds, you will be aware that there is a separation between the part of us that can absorb knowledge like a sponge, and the organizational part of us that gives us a hard time, makes us feel bad and thus closes up our learning channels. You may also be aware that in a battle between the conscious and the unconscious, the unconscious will win every time. How many times have you tried really hard to behave in a certain way in a particular situation, and blown it none the less? Later, we are going to explore ways of getting our act together. In the meantime I want to tell you a story.

> Once upon a time, in a far away land, there lived a prosperous people. They prospered because they had a great treasure as security. This great treasure was an enormous and beautiful antique gold coin – the only one of its kind in the whole world, and the envy of all the neighbouring lands. And the people knew that if ever they needed to borrow money when times were hard, their treasure was worth a million times more than any amount they might need to borrow.
>
> The treasure was kept in the palace on a scarlet velvet cushion. And because each side of the golden coin was a work of art in its own right and in order that the people could fully enjoy their treasure, the ceremonial Turning of the Coin took place every day, and people came from miles around to enjoy the occasion, and to see and touch their treasure.
>
> And times changed, as times do; the land evolved, new fashions came in and maybe the people got bored with being prosperous – I don't know; all I do know is that they began to quarrel because some preferred one side of the coin and some preferred the other, and neither party could understand why their favourite side should not be permanently on display.
>
> So they sent for the Grand Adviser who, for a vast fee, pronounced that the coin should be cut in half; so that both works of art could be displayed at the same time, side by side. This was duly done. The two halves were housed in a new, glorious display cabinet, and the expensive, time-wasting Turning of the Coin ceremony was no more.
>
> When the bad times came again, the people went to a

neighbouring kingdom to borrow some money, as they had always done. The neighbours sent round the Grand Valuer to inspect the treasure, as they had always done. And when the Grand Valuer discovered that the coin had been defaced, he explained to the people that their treasure was now only worth its weight in gold, which was not sufficient security to cover the amount that they wanted to borrow.

For a long time the people argued with each other about what was the best thing to do and about who was to blame. And there was misery throughout the land until one day the Magician appeared. This Magician's speciality was gold: he knew everything there was to know about it, and how to weave spells that would restore the coin to its original state, so that even the Grand Valuer would believe that he had been dreaming when he had seen it in two halves.

The Magician went into the Coin Room alone and gave orders that he was not to be disturbed. And I do not know what spells he wove; I do not know whether he stayed awake or went to sleep; all I know is that when he came out of the Coin Room the next morning, the people found their treasure suspended in thin air – as if hanging from an invisible thread – so that both sides were on view to delight and entrance everybody. And the more they gazed at and touched their beloved treasure, the more the people became aware of how much they preferred it in its original state, and the more pleased, delighted and relieved they felt. And there was great rejoicing and feasting throughout the land, and from that moment on they became the greatest people the world has ever known, and they all lived happily ever after.

WHAT WE LEARN

We learn all sorts of extraordinary things, which may bear no relationship to what we are 'supposed' to learn. There was a little boy who could not read whose parents brought him a computer. The parents knew nothing about computers, so this little boy taught himself to read from the computer handbook. Nobody told him that computer handbooks were much too difficult for him to understand, so he just got on with it because he wanted to know how to work the machine. There are supposedly mentally retarded people who have learned to do the most unusual things (which you or I probably could not do), which for some reason have grabbed their interest – like the brothers who could look at a huge pile of matches and tell you immediately and correctly how many there were. And NLP-ers would tell you that there is nothing in this book that you did not know already, deep down inside you. However, because you were probably unable to prove most of it in logical terms, no one paid any attention to your ideas. For example, you have probably always known that something deep inside you sometimes stops you from being your best or standing up for yourself, but it is only relatively recently that people have started to pay attention to theories with such a lack of objectivity.

We learn about things in our immediate surroundings: what happens if we smile; what happens when we pull the cat's tail; what happens if we touch something hot. In *Nurtured by Love* Professor Shinichi Suzuki, who created the famous Talent Education Research Institute in Tokyo, describes how very young children learn to play the violin: a parent plays the violin; they want to be just like that parent, so they pick up the miniature violin that just happens to be lying around and have a go. He tells us how three-year-old Hitomi would play her violin for three hours a day, as if it were a toy. Three- to five-year-olds trained by Suzuki have performed in concerts around the world.

We learn to do things that make us feel good, and things that we like. A young client was having terrible trouble with reading. I checked where she had filed it in her brain; was it in the 'Like' or 'Dislike' file? When I discovered it was in 'Dislike', I asked her what would happen if she put it into her 'Like' file. She looked at me as though I were a complete idiot and said, with more than a hint of impatience; 'Well, then I'd like it, wouldn't I?' And how did she know what would happen? She put it into the 'Like' file and her feelings changed immediately. Your brain is so obliging, that it really is that easy. There may, of course, be very powerful reasons for not liking a subject, in which case you may not want to change files just yet; we will discuss these reasons in 'About Not Learning' and there will be more about your filing system in 'Some Tricks of the Trade'.

We learn that vocalizing makes us feel better. As newborn babies we are in the survival business, so we need to arrange for our creature comforts to be provided. We are lying quietly in our cots, experiencing, watching and listening to what is going on around us when we become aware that we are hungry or wet. We stop listening and start to cry and someone comes to the rescue. We have just learned that making a noise is more productive than listening – the end result of making a noise is that we feel better – and many of us retain a subconscious belief that talking will produce better feelings than listening.

We learn to interrupt so that we can talk instead of listen. A most effective way of doing this is to pay attention to irrelevant detail rather than the whole message, so that, for example, we can leap upon a possible mistake and argue about it. Once again, this is nothing to do with the speaker personally; we just need to feel better. By the end of the discussion, if the speaker is sufficiently tenacious to get to the end, we have taken in none of the message, but we may remember until our dying day that the idiot Bloggs said the wind was coming from the east, simply because we made such an effort to interrupt him in order to feel good.

We learn that committing our whole neurology to a discussion makes us feel good. When we raise our voices, wave our arms and move about, we are releasing adrenalin. I remember driving 100 miles with my sons while they argued all the way. It was not until later that I realized that, in spite of the insults they were hurling at one another, they were actually enjoying themselves. Hurling insults is great; feeling that we have won is great: our unconscious need to feel good is satisfied – however, we may not consider the effect that our words may have on other people.

We learn to observe other members of the family system. When we are children, these are the people in charge of our survival, and we need to know what is going on. We might learn that when father has a certain look on his face, there is likely to be trouble; that when mother feels tense as she holds us, this is the prelude to a terrible argument; that when we hear a certain tone of voice, we are about to be punished. And because we know in advance what is going to happen, we feel bad. This develops into a precarious cause-and-effect program: when father looks like that, I feel bad. If we are unaware of what is happening, this program may last us for the rest of our lives, not only with father, but with anyone else who has that look on his or her face.

We learn the dangerous art of mind-reading. Mother is angry: we have seen the frown on her face, read her mind and decided that this is so. Mother is actually frowning because she has a headache and is feeling very fragile, but we consider ourselves so good at mind-reading that this possibility never comes into our heads; mother is angry, it must be my fault, I feel bad.

We learn to blame other people. We believe that if a parent discovers who really broke the plate, they might stop loving us and, at best, stop looking after us; at worst, abandon us. It is much safer to blame someone else. There is nothing personal in this, we have nothing against the person we are blaming; we are just satisfying our unconscious need to protect ourselves.

We learn what is bad about us. Ian McDermott, an NLP trainer, was invited by a colleague to visit his classroom. When he was asked to hand out the corrected homework, Ian noticed it was covered in red ink. Trying not to display his horror at an excess of criticism, he enquired what all the red ink was about, and received the casual reply: 'Oh, we only underline what is right'. What a concept! I wonder what difference it would have made to us all if we had only been told what was right about us, instead of what was wrong.

I suppose it takes too long for us to tell each other what is good, so we choose to save time by listing everything that we consider to be bad. For example, if I were to list everything that is good about you, it would take a long time; it would be much quicker to point out that your hair is untidy or that I do not like whatever colour you are wearing. And, maybe, if I can produce an adverse criticism of Snooks that you have not thought of, I am 'one up' on you for a change, and this will make me feel good.

Robert Dilts and Todd Epstein, of the NLP University in California, have their own concept of criticism: *Catch someone doing something right and tell them*. This method produces star performers. Students know that the result of having their work observed is that they will hear something good about themselves, so instead of being on edge for fear of adverse criticism, they can enjoy their work and do it beautifully. They also discover all sorts of nice things about themselves that they were not aware of.

We learn to get attention. We need to be acknowledged as individual members of the system. We can achieve this by doing all the right things and pleasing the powers that be, or by doing all the wrong things and displeasing them; either way we get attention, because what we have done is acknowledged. Maybe the only way we can get attention is by deliberately doing something awful.

A useful attention getter is 'Why?'. Have you had one of those discussions with a child recently? 'Why?' guarantees that the other person will go on talking to you, at least until they get bored. It is much more effective than 'No', and it requires less effort. A young acquaintance of mine used to announce 'It's my birthday today' to everyone who came to the house, thereby guaranteeing instant, total attention from each visitor.

We learn to model other people. In order to become part of the family system we need to be able to behave like other members of it. The simplest way of doing this is to model people. We may take on a role model lock, stock and barrel: little boys can be seen looking and behaving exactly like their fathers, and little girls, just like their mothers. I remember being horrified by the tone of voice a small girl used to address her mother until I realized that that was exactly the same tone that her father used when talking to her mother.

In *Nurtured by Love* Professor Suzuki tells us that children who had been brought up by wolves were faster on four legs than a human on two; they developed grotesquely large heads; they used their mouths to pick things up; they could see in the dark; they grew thick hair on their chests and shoulders; they panted instead of sweating.

Modelling can produce some interesting beliefs, such as: I can't do maths, because my mother can't do maths; I am an alcoholic because my father was an alcoholic.

We learn strategies for doing things. Good communicators have learned how to join other people in their models of the world; good leaders have learned how to get the best from each member of their team; good doctors have learned how to treat each patient as the most important person in the world. None of these people may be consciously aware of what they do and how they do it, but they all employ effective strategies. As children we may learn that if we shout at people who take our toys, people will stop taking our toys. Later, we may find that if we lose our temper, we can get our way, or if we get angry, people will not dare to argue with us. These, too, are effective, but there may be better ways of doing things, which are more compatible with who we are now.

I suspect that most of us hit upon our strategies quite by chance. We try something and get a result. If it achieves our unconscious outcome, we will go on using this strategy even if it is inappropriate. If it does not work, we may decide we cannot do whatever we tried, because we are unaware that there are other ways of doing things. You can compare strategies to computer software. The brains we were born with are like computer hardware: a machine. The strategies we use are like computer software: programs that we can buy to do specialized things. For example, my computer is not a word-processor, so I am using word-processing software to put my thoughts on paper. The software is the 'how'. Success in intelligence tests proves only one thing: you know how to do intelligence tests; you have the software, the strategy. Failure in intelligence tests simply means that you do not have the software, and therefore you do not know how to do the tests. And the useful thing about software is that we can update it at any time.

We learn to give ourselves a hard time. *Sit still! Concentrate! Listen! Pay attention! Try harder!* All this increases the stress and closes our learning channels. John Grinder asks an interesting question: 'Why do we talk about paying attention as though it costs us something?'

I was playing 'hangman' with some Russian children who knew very little English. We had just read *Dr Seuss's ABC* and Igor had chosen 'rhinoceros' as his word. Vera got bored because it was not her turn and it was taking too long, so she went off round the corner to play. A few minutes later she came running back, saying, 'I know! I know! Rhinoceros!' She had not been paying any attention at all, but she got the answer.

We learn not to be too clever. For some extraordinary reason some of us do not seem to approve of success. If someone is doing well, there will be a collection of vultures hanging around, gleefully waiting for disaster to strike. Perhaps because we are so determined to fit in with the system, many of us make less of ourselves so as not to appear more important than anyone else.

I asked a client who was having trouble at work what he would lose if he got on better with his superiors, and the answer was 'my friends'. He was the office buffoon, and kept his colleagues rocking in the aisles. Losing our friends is not something we want to do: it is our friends who give us the acknowledgement and attention that we need. My client then had to think how success would affect him. He realized that, of course, he could be successful *and* funny, thereby achieving both his objectives.

We learn to protect ourselves emotionally. We may keep away from other people, thus guaranteeing that they cannot hurt us. We may put up an invisible barrier so that people cannot get too close. We may lash out physically or verbally at anyone who makes us feel bad. We may belittle other people in order to make ourselves feel bigger. We may behave aggressively to keep other people away. Whatever we do, and however inappropriate it may be, the positive intention is to protect ourselves from harm. And because mistakes are part of the learning process, we can ask our unconscious mind to think of a more appropriate way to do this; a way with which we can feel more comfortable and still be safe from harm.

I discovered that the unconscious arrangement I had made for my protection was like barbed wire, which is nasty and dangerous – it goes rusty and can poison people. Now I have an imaginary electric fence instead. It is about a foot off the ground and all my friends can see it and step over it; anyone who wishes me harm cannot see it, so they get zapped automatically. The system is permanently in place, and now I never have to worry about protecting myself. This may sound crazy, but it works.

Some people agree immediately with my theory that most of us feel inadequate quite a lot of the time; some people say that *they* feel inadequate, but they do not think that other people do; and some people will look me straight in the eye and tell me forcefully that they *never* feel inadequate.

We learn to judge. Our 'elders and betters' pronounce things good or bad, right or wrong. As small people we have no other point of reference and so the way that we do things in our family, school, class, group or culture must be the right way. It follows, therefore, that anyone or anything that does not conform to what we know must be wrong or bad, and this deduction may have been made at a very deep, unconscious level. We only have to listen to Sir Humphrey Appleby in *Yes, Prime Minister* saying blandly, 'Well, it's been done this way for three hundred years, therefore it must be right' to realize how insidious our programming is; and it is useful to remember Hamlet: 'There is nothing either good or bad, but thinking makes it so.'

Unconscious modelling of parents goes on in all aspects of our lives, for example, suffering from the same diseases, losing our hair, or even abusing children mentally or physically: 'My father beat me, this must therefore be how fathers behave.'

WHERE AND WHEN WE LEARN

These are individual questions. Some people learn best when they are sitting up, others when they are lying down. Some people can read more fluently when they are moving about. Some people learn best in the morning, some in the afternoon, some in the evening. Some learn best when sitting on a particular colour. Where and when do you learn best? There are no right or wrong answers – there are only your answers.

We learn in safe, supportive surroundings. We learn when we are feeling relaxed and good about ourselves. The small child in familiar surroundings, exploring a world where it feels safe, in the midst of an encouraging family, is learning all the time without being aware of it. We are doing the same when we are having fun with a hobby or pastime we enjoy. There is nothing to make us feel bad, so all our learning channels are open.

We learn when all our neurology is engaged in the process. If we can see, hear, feel, taste and smell what we are learning about, we will remember it. If it involves our emotions, we will remember it: if it is funny or unusual, we will remember it; if it is frightening, we will remember it (which is probably why we learn so many of the unhelpful things, we were talking about earlier).

I once found a very respectable French friend tearing round her kitchen at nine o'clock in the morning, flinging open cupboards and drawers, and shrieking '*Où est le scotch?*' It was not until she triumphantly produced a roll of sticky tape and began to wrap a parcel that I realized that she had not suddenly turned into an alcoholic. I was so involved in the drama, that I shall always remember this piece of vocabulary.

We learn when we are allowed to do so in our own way. One client learned everything through his body, and schoolwork was a disaster because he was expected to produce answers to problems he could only *see* on the blackboard – he could not feel them. Another client was told that her strategy for doing addition was 'wrong' even though she was producing the right answers; this strange reasoning was beyond her, so she decided that addition was beyond her as well.

We learn when our conscious mind is distracted. I learned most of my French either while riding a horse or playing bridge, and in general conversation. My conscious mind was on the horse, the cards or my companions, leaving my unconscious to get on with learning French without any interference from the part of me that worries about making mistakes.

Most of us learn best when our right ear is towards the speaker. A client used to sit with her left ear towards the trainer until she discovered this. She moved to the other side of the room to see what would happen, and found that the information went in much more easily. A colleague told me how her elderly mother-in-law always turned her 'bad' ear towards a speaker who was saying something she did not want to hear. Which ear do you listen with, and when?

We find it easier to reproduce facts in the place where we learned them. In order to ensure that we can reproduce knowledge somewhere else, it is useful to ask the unconscious mind to take it out into the world with us. Sometimes we learn strategies for doing things in one situation and do not apply them in another. There are people who have brilliant relationships at work and do not bring their strategies home to use with their families; we hear of hospital doctors who cannot treat members of their own family until they have driven them to the hospital and put on a white coat. The trick with new learning is to ask your unconscious mind to apply it in any situation where it might be useful.

We learn when I'm OK and you're OK. The psychologist Eric Berne created the concept of OK-ness. If you are trying to teach me something, and I think that I am OK but you are not, I probably won't pay much attention to you, because I do not consider that you will have anything important to say. If I think that you are OK but I am not, I may decide that whatever you have to offer will be way above my head, so there is not much point in my listening to you. If I decide that neither of us is OK, there is no point at all in listening to you – you have nothing to offer, and I cannot learn anyway. However, if I know that I am OK and you are OK, I am aware that we each have a lot to offer the other and we are going to have an interesting discussion.

$$HIJKLMNO = H \text{ to } O = H_2O = \text{water}.$$
What did you dream about?

What did you discover about you and your learning? You might like to make a list that is personal to you in answer to the questions where, when, what, how, why and who?

About Not Learning

WHERE AND WHEN WE DO NOT LEARN

Because we are all unique, we will find lots of different examples of the circumstances in which we do not learn. For example, some people cannot engage their brains in the morning; some late at night; some people cannot learn without gallons of coffee; some people cannot learn in a classroom situation because it reminds them too much of school. The common denominator of all these situations is: where and when we feel bad or uncomfortable. So let us think about what can contribute to making us feel bad.

When we are aware of what is making us feel bad, it is easy to change things. I know that I cannot learn effectively after a large lunch; I just feel fat and full and I want to go to sleep. I also know that I cannot learn effectively if I have to sit still for too long, so every twenty minutes or so I get up and move about. I know that my eyes get tired if I look at the computer screen for too long, so every now and then I look away and deliberately lengthen my vision. All these wheres and whens are personal to me; where and when do you not learn effectively?

Places and things

A client told me in despair that she just could not learn French. We discovered that the trigger for her bad feelings was the smell of chalk in the classroom, which took her unwittingly straight back to school, where she had been a disaster. However, she now has a very complicated job, which she loves and knows she does well, so there is no question of a lack of belief in her own intelligence. We compared the pictures that she had in her mind's eye of her work and the French class, and discovered the differences: when she thought about work, it was all going on around her, life size, in colour, as though she were really there; when she thought about her French class, she saw a picture of herself in the classroom in black and white, and she saw that she was very small in proportion to the rest of the picture. No wonder she felt bad. She changed the pictures to life size, colour; and so on, so that she felt that she was really there, in the classroom, learning French, and the bad feelings were replaced by the good feelings that she has when she is at work. Although she was initially unaware of what was making her feel bad, once we found out, it was easily remedied. You will find out more about these techniques in 'Some Tricks of the Trade'.

Other people

You may think you cannot learn a certain subject because you felt bad when you were with a particular teacher. Here is another experiment for you to try.

Imagine that you can see that person in black and white on a television screen on the other side of the room. Once you have got used to the fact that the person is trapped in the TV, start to speed up the film, until he or she looks and behaves like Charlie Chaplin and sounds like the Chipmunks. Then speed up the film even more; make it go faster and faster until you know that, having seen that person behaving so ridiculously, you can only laugh when you think of him or her.

Ourselves

The conscious mind has a great power to make us feel bad, with its insistence upon trying, working hard, controlling ourselves, concentrating! We even tell ourselves to *try* to relax, which is as crazy a contradiction in terms as we could wish. Trying is very trying.

The left brain controls the right side of the body. The left brain also has words at its disposal. It is interesting to think about how 'right' is assumed to be good.

- That's right!
- An upright man
- That's all right.
- Right you are!
- Right away!
- Righteous.
- The right way.

Whereas *left* comes from an Old English word meaning weak or feeble. *Gauche*, the French word for 'left' can also mean clumsy or distorted; as can the Spanish word *izquierdo*. English has taken *sinister*, the Latin word for 'left' and turned it into something malevolent. French uses it to mean dark or gloomy, or to say that disaster has struck. Left, as my mother used to say, is definitely not right. Once we are aware of this bias in favour of right and recognize that we live in a culture of words, it is hardly surprising that the right brain, which controls the left side of the body and has no words, is largely ignored. And if people can run rings around each other with words, think what the left brain can do to the right brain without our being consciously aware of it.

When we are completely absorbed in a task, we may suddenly become aware at a conscious level that we are doing it rather well and, as soon as the conscious mind gets in on the act, it likes to try to take over. One of the ways that it does this is by warning us of potential dangers ahead; for example,

'Well, you've done OK so far, but how long do you think you will be able to keep it up? Now this bit is particularly difficult – be careful, otherwise you'll mess it up. You've never been able to do this next bit properly, you're so stupid! *Try!*' And thus our relaxed internal state is lost.

Betty Edwards, a professor of art at California State University, whose research into brain function and drawing has led to demand for her workshops from leading businesses and research organizations around the world, explains in *Drawing on the Right Side of the Brain* and *Drawing on the Artist Within* her theory that some people cannot draw because drawing is a right-brained occupation and while the left brain is insisting on getting in on the act, the right brain cannot do its stuff. She gets people to draw things upside down and eventually the left brain gets bored with working out what something *should* look like when it is the wrong way up and gives up the struggle, leaving the right brain to draw in peace.

When I was learning to ski, I was all alone on a lovely, easy slope – all alone except for one man, who was some way down the slope. 'You must not *ski into him*', said my conscious mind, so I concentrated really hard on not *skiing into him*. I tried, and I tried and I tried, and I skied straight into him.

And now I want you to do something very important to set yourself up for the next exercise. It is essential that you get this right, before you go on: *try not to think of the colour purple*. Do not, under any circumstances, think of the colour purple.

As you have just discovered, in order not to think of something, you have to think of it – otherwise you have no reference point for what you are not supposed to be thinking about.

Pressure and stress

When I was on a teacher training course we were told that the *right* way to ask questions was: '*Pose ... Pause – Pounce*'.

You have to keep students on their toes, otherwise they'll go to sleep; so you pose the question, you pause and then you *pounce* on someone for the answer. We practised this assiduously, and I could not do it. It was not until later that I realized that the reason I could not do it was because my unconscious mind would not allow me to do it; I had never treated my unfortunate students like that before, so why should I start now? Sean could not do it either, so I told him my new theory. He was worried about assessment, so he went on practising until he got it right.

Assessment time came, and Sean was giving us a wonderful lesson. I was enjoying every moment, until a little voice said, 'He's going to ask you a question.' Sure enough, Sean posed his question, he paused and then he pounced on me; and my mind went completely blank. I could imagine the assessor at the back of the room writing: 'Explanations not sufficiently clear: Diana could not answer question', and I was covered in shame for having let Sean down. Now, if this could happen to me when I knew exactly what was going on, what happens to innocents in the classroom when they are put under pressure? And what does teacher think of little Johnnie when he cannot answer a perfectly simple question? What does the rest of the class think? Little Johnnie is written off as stupid.

Even as adults we are quite capable of regressing to childhood in a classroom situation and feeling that that Know-All over there is trying to be one up on us at every turn, or that that ghastly woman with the winsome smile is trying to become teacher's pet or that everybody else seems to know more about the subject than we do and therefore that everyone else must think we are stupid. Then, in an effort to prove that we are not stupid, we may say something completely idiotic, and make ourselves feel even worse. Out of the classroom, if we feel under pressure, or if somebody makes us feel small we may not take in a word they are saying. This can also happen if we feel we are being bullied or that someone is trying to force their opinions onto us.

Modal operators (Should/ought to/must)

I am contrary by nature and if you tell me that I should, ought to or must do something, I am likely to do the exact opposite; the technical term for people like me is 'polarity responder'. While most people are more obliging than I am, I do not believe that a load of shoulds, ought tos and musts makes anybody feel good, so I have devised a scheme for my clients, which is going to make me very rich: every time they use one of these modal operators on someone else, they owe me £5; every time they use one on themselves, they owe me £20. I also rope in their families, promising them a 10 per cent cut for telling tales.

One of my polarity-responder friends was determined to hang on to his illusion that life was too awful for words, so I wrote him a letter telling him that he should, ought to, must think about all the things I did not want him to think about, and that he should not, ought not to and must not think about all the things that I did want him to think about. My husband, unaware of the master plan, considered the letter extremely pompous and patronizing, which was the exact effect that I wanted. It worked a treat.

WHAT WE DO NOT LEARN

In my work with academic subjects mathematics seems to be a major contender in the poll of things that we do not learn, and we may decide that as maths is classed as a science, we will put physics, chemistry and biology into the same category. When reading, writing, and spelling are also on this list, it seriously affects our own, and other people's, beliefs about our capabilities.

As adults, some of us establish our filters so firmly before we start that we only learn what we expect to learn. For example, if we 'know' that women are bad drivers, we will not notice and be interested by any good women drivers; if we are only looking for techniques, all we will see is techniques and the rationale behind them will escape us completely. We will learn the tricks of the trade and never stop to wonder about the thinking that created them. For chess players, the queen is the most powerful piece on the board; and I wonder how many players make the connection between her power and her flexibility, and use this knowledge in their lives by becoming more flexible and thus more powerful.

We do not learn things that are of no use to us. Einstein did not learn his own telephone number, because he could not foresee an occasion when he would need to telephone himself. If we cannot make a connection between the information and how it will benefit us, we do not learn it: as I do not foresee a time when I might take up tiddleywinks, there is no point in my learning the rules of the game.

We do not learn what is not interesting. Despite what I have just said, I am a mine of useless information, like how *pommes soufflées* were discovered (I am interested in food and in quirks of fate) or that William Shakespeare apparently left no books in his will (I find this curious). But it is no good asking me about the latest scandal in high places, because any information I was given went in one ear and out the other.

We do not learn things that we dislike. Some of us have hung on to our loathing for figures so effectively that we cannot get promotion because we do not learn anything related to figures in the workplace. Some of us dislike learning foreign languages and thus miss out on valuable export business.

We do not learn things that are presented in our least-used system. Read me a piece of civil service gobbledygook and I will go straight into a trance. Telling me how a machine works without showing me and then letting me play with it is a complete waste of time, whereas for primarily auditory people verbal instructions will be perfect.

Like the wheres and whens, the whats are very individual, and it is the whys that are important. Think about the things that you do not learn: which category do they fit into? And can you discover any more categories for yourself?

HOW WE DO NOT LEARN

Before we start this section, I would like you to do an intelligence test, which can be done by the average twelve year-old in twenty seconds. I want you to find out how much faster you can do it, so set your watch and record the time.

> 1. I like Puccini less than Verdi.
> 2. I dislike Wagner less than Britten.
> 3. I don't enjoy Donizetti as much as Puccini.
> 4. I dislike Wagner more than Donizetti.
>   Which composer do I like least?
> When the twenty seconds are up, you can read on.

I apologize for telling you the only deliberate lie in this book: it would take the average twelve-year-old twenty minutes, rather than twenty seconds, to solve that puzzle. I also apologize for putting you through the ordeal. I first came across this idea in *The Alpha Plan*, by the psychologist, lecturer and broadcaster Dr David Lewis. When I discovered that he had deliberately set me up, I nearly threw the book in the fire. But then I realized that I had just learned something important: I had learned what happened to me when I was under stress. What happened to you? You might like to write down your different reactions and then, when you have finished, get up, move around and do whatever you need to do to shake off all those bad feelings. For example, what happened to:

- your head?
- your vision and internal pictures?
- your hearing and internal dialogue?
- your mouth, your tongue, your saliva?
- your throat and your ability to swallow?
- your neck and shoulders?
- your breathing?
- your heart rate?
- your stomach?
- any other part of you?

What triggered off this collection of reactions? Was it the idea of an intelligence test? Was it the thought of doing it against the clock? Was it the fear of not being able to do it as fast as a twelve-year-old? Some people at the workshops I run say it was because they wanted to please me. They admit that this is crazy, but the need to please others is something we learn early in life. David Lewis really piles on the agony: he pounces on people and if they get the answer right, demands, 'Are you sure or are you just guessing?' I sometimes do that to parents who are giving their children a hard time, having already primed the child to create as much distraction as possible during the twenty seconds so that the parents can experience how it feels to be put under stress. Some people's hands shake so much that they cannot unfold the test paper; a lot of people find that their vision is so badly affected that they cannot even finish reading the question in the time; I got such a loud burbling in my ears that my brain refused to function at all because I could not hear myself think. And the fascinating thing about all this is that we create it ourselves. We manage to stop ourselves from learning, when learning is something that is second nature to us.

Displacement activity

This is an effective technique. It requires endless ingenuity to divert our own and other people's attention from something we do not want to do. Here are some ideas from a client in response to the mention of fractions:

- The cat wants to go out. Can I let it out?
- I can't find my pencil.
- There's a helicopter coming over. Can I take a photograph?
- Can I get a drink of water?
- My pencil is blunt. Can I sharpen it?
- The cat wants to come in again. Can I let it in?

Listen to the irrelevancies that come up in discussions, or to people concentrating on picking tiny holes in your ideas because your big plan might make life difficult for them.

Blocking one or more learning channels

As you saw, my strategy for not learning is to create noises in my ears. Normally, I use my ears as an open learning channel, simply allowing sounds to pour in so that I can convert them into pictures and then feelings. The noises I create in my ears when I am under stress instantly alert the rest of the system to go on the blink, because it cannot make any pictures from a terrible noise.

When life is good for Caroline, everything smells nice; under stress, the nice smell switches off, immediately alerting the rest of her senses to close down. Sylvain is aware of his own internal rhythm when things are going well; under threat, he can no longer feel it, so the alarm bells start to ring. What wondrously clever device do you employ in order to guarantee that your learning channels will close down?

And while you think about that, remember that your unconscious mind has nothing but positive intentions for you; it quite properly wants to protect you, and protect you it will – whatever happens. As I told you, I know that cats protect my garden from elephants, because I have always had a cat and there have never been any elephants in my garden. Similarly, your unconscious mind has proof that your protection system works, because you are still alive. The only question I would ask of your unconscious mind is, is there a better way to protect you?

We take in everything that is around us through our five senses. In order not to take in pain, which includes stress, the simplest solution is to close down all five senses. A less drastic solution is to reduce input, which may mean black-and-white pictures and distorted sound. Some people live exclusively in their heads, and experience no feelings at all, which keeps pain out very efficiently. The disadvantage of this strategy is that they have deprived themselves of an entire learning channel, and there is no place for joy either.

So what would be the most efficient, most comfortable, most productive protection system for you? You might like to allow your unconscious mind to work on this by itself, knowing that it has nothing but your best interests at heart; you could simply explain what you want and allow it to do the rest in its own time and in its own way.

Your unconscious mind will do anything you ask. I never write shopping lists and one day my husband told me that we had run out of paper tissues, while I was busy with something else and did not want to be distracted; I simply asked my unconscious to remind me of paper tissues when I went shopping, and went on with what I was doing. Later, as I was wandering round the supermarket, trying to remember what on earth he had asked me to buy, my nose started to run. On another occasion we had run out of light bulbs. On my way to the supermarket I selected, apparently at random, one of the tapes by Robert Dilts and Todd Epstein to play in the car. As I arrived at the supermarket, Robert Dilts started to tell light bulb jokes. My unconscious knows how cross my husband gets if I forget things (he thinks I should write lists), so it arranges my life accordingly.

WHY WE DO NOT LEARN

We believe that we are stupid. The curious thing about this belief is that it has been inflicted upon us by somebody else. We would have no concept of stupidity if someone had not told us about it and applied the adjective to us. 'Don't be stupid', 'What a silly thing to say', 'What a stupid thing to do!' and so on. 'Sticks and stones may break my bones, but words will never hurt me' – not true! Words can hurt, and the memory of them sticks, although we may pretend not to be affected. Even when people do not use the word 'stupid', their manner gives them away: we pick up all their subconscious signals when we fail to answer a question, as they smile kindly and move on to someone seemingly more intelligent.

We choose not to learn. There are the usual reasons for choosing not to do something; for example, 'it's boring'; 'there's nothing in it for me'; 'I have not got that amount of time to invest'. These may all be conscious choices, and are up to the individual. Then there are the unconscious choices, which are the most interesting.

A bad experience with the subject. Pierre was fifteen and still in a class of ten-year-olds because of his low marks in mathematics. I asked him how long he had hated maths: 'Always' came the firm reply. So we watched an imaginary film of the beginning of his schooldays (Pierre is very visual), and he was surprised to discover that, in fact, he had enjoyed maths then. We fast fowarded the film until he suddenly said, 'I see! I see!', and what he saw in his mind's eye was himself at the age of ten in a maths class, painstakingly doing his work when he suddenly noticed that there was something stuck in the nib of his fountain pen, which had left an inky trail on the paper. He put the pen down to look at the mess. At that moment the teacher walked over to him, took the pen and, saying 'What on earth are you doing?', shook it at Pierre, and the ink flew out all over his face.

You can imagine his poor unconscious mind trying to compute this: 'I take pains with my maths, and I get ink thrown in my face. This gives me a shock, humiliates me in front of my classmates and makes me feel bad. If that is what happens when I take pains, I had better stop taking pains at once.' So that was what he did. His unconscious evidence procedure that this was a good strategy was to wait and see if anyone threw more ink in his face. Nobody did, so, by default, he had proof positive that the plan was working. After we had replayed the movie enough times for Pierre to take a detached view of the situation, he realized that the teacher had not meant to throw ink in his face, and that he was, in fact, mortified. From then on I could not stop him. We used Cuisenaire Rods (see page 120). Pierre could see what he was doing, and enjoyed the beauty and elegance of mathematics so much that he would still be searching for patterns, and trying different ways of doing things long after I was bored.

Someone makes us feel bad. We can probably all remember similar occasions and can review them with the detachment of time. Bad experiences that we are aware of and detached from are reasonably easy to put behind us. It is when we are unaware of the insidious effect of other people's behaviour towards us that we may not be able to do anything about it.

In an experiment schoolchildren were given an IQ test at the beginning of the school year. Afterwards, the researchers arbitrarily divided the children into two classes without looking at the results, telling the teachers confidentially that the children in Class A were the more intelligent. I have no doubt that the teachers kept the secret, but because Class A's teacher believed that those children were the bright ones, she treated them as such; and, of course, Class B's teacher had no expectations of the 'less intelligent' children, and treated them accordingly. At the end of the year the children were given another IQ test. This time it was marked. The children in Class A did far better than the children in Class B. They had picked up the subconscious messages that their teachers were sending them about their expectations, and so they lived up to those expectations.

Try this experiment from John Grinder on your friends. It is for two people, and neither is aware of the instructions given to the other.

1. A and B were at school together, and they meet again after a number of years. Talk for ten minutes. Each writes down his or her impressions of the other.

2. Instructions for A: you knew B x number of years ago, when he or she had lots of money and was flashing it about everywhere. He or she ran over your dog/cat, and treated it as a huge joke.

   Instructions for B: x number of years ago A ran off with your brother's wife/sister's husband, leaving a destroyed family, money problems and so on.

   A and B now find themselves sitting next to each

other at a meeting, waiting for proceedings to start. They talk for ten minutes. Each writes down his or her impressions of the other.

I did this exercise with Simon, whom I had not met before. After the first part, I wrote down that he was intelligent, amusing and fun. After the second part, I wrote that he was disagreeable, boring and arrogant. How could I have reached such totally different conclusions about the same person? It was not until that moment that I truly became aware of how presuppositions about another person can affect our internal state, and how our internal state can affect our communication.

We are not allowed to learn in our own way. An educational psychologist told me about a boy who was expelled from school for cheating because he would not write down his arithmetical calculations; he preferred to do them all in his head, tapping with his index finger as he worked things out. The more complicated the calculations became, the less the authorities could believe that he really was doing it all in his head and because he refused to tell them how he was cheating, they expelled him. This is an extreme example of not being allowed to do things in our own way.

A delightful story is told by the American educationalist John Holt in *How Children Learn*. He had spent weeks fruitlessly trying to teach his class how to calculate what weights would balance on a set of scales. Eventually he gave up, put the scales in a corner of the room and did not mention them again. It was then that the children began to play with them, and in no time at all they had taught themselves exactly how the scales worked and what they needed to do to balance them.

We are discouraged from original thought. Can you remember – I can, very clearly – asking what seemed to you to be a very important, if not profound, question and being brushed aside or told not to be silly? Original thinkers must be the bane of parents' and teachers' lives. Asking questions they cannot answer is not the way to endear ourselves to people who are not very sure of their ground. David Lewis talks about various inventive thinkers: the child who built a hot-air balloon and was about to send the family cat up into space; the child whose ham radio tuned in to the most secret of networks – such an embarrassment with the police coming round! We need to understand why people reacted to us the way that they did in order to let go of that reaction and its effects on us and return to our innocent, questing questioning when faced with being stopped in our tracks by statements like 'You can't do that!' 'What would happen if I did?' makes the speaker stop and think. If there is a good enough reason, like 'Your car could be towed away', we can accept it; if not, we have laid the ground for negotiation.

We are taught to reproduce other people's ideas, not our own. When someone for whom I had the greatest respect pronounced, about twelve years ago, that I was incapable of original thought, I accepted it cheerfully, because that was what I believed about myself. I am still surprised when I make a discovery about something that is apparently entirely new. Once I was talking to a special needs teacher who believed he was infinitely superior to me. I allowed him to tell me that as I had not had any special needs training, I had nothing to offer the children with whom he worked. He was not interested in my discovery about how people see letters and words back to front (which you will find in Some Tricks of the Trade).

I suspect that, for many of us, if we have a problem with a theory or a philosophy or a popularly held belief, we probably blame ourselves, thinking that if there is something that we have not understood properly: *it must be our fault.* And I wonder what would happen if you allowed your mind the freedom to question all those things that you always thought were not *quite* right.

We are discouraged from maintaining our natural openness and curiosity. Personal remarks and questions about matters that have nothing to do with us are not considered good manners in our society:

- You've got a big spot on the end of your nose.
- How old are you? (To anyone over thirty.)
- Why has that man got a silly voice?
- Why are you wearing those funny clothes?

From the reactions of those around us to what we say, we rapidly pick up the information that openness and curiosity may displease. Consequently, we may give up observation altogether and stop asking questions in order to ensure that the people upon whom we depend will continue to love us.

We have not got the software. We can think of our learning hardware in terms of the millions of millions of available connections between our brain cells, between a single thought and interconnections of thoughts, rather like the worldwide telephone networks that are being generated and improved upon all the time. It is in place and is always available to us. The software provides the information that enables us to do something specific, whether it is to tie a shoelace or fly a helicopter. For example, because I am not a plumber, I have not invested in plumbing software. The software for David Lewis's intelligence test is beautifully simple, and you could have worked it out for yourself if I had not put you under so much pressure. Imagine that each sentence in turn gives the answer to the question 'Which composer do I like least?'

1. I like Puccini less than Verdi. *Answer: Puccini.*
2. I dislike Wagner less than Britten: this changes nothing yet, so move on.
3. I don't enjoy Donizetti as much as Puccini. *Answer: Donizetti.*
4. I dislike Wagner more than Donizetti. *Answer: Wagner.*

Now you can go back to No. 2.

2. I dislike Wagner less than Britten. *Answer: Britten.*

To demonstrate to yourself just how simple the problem is, now that you have the software, which composer do I like best? You will find more software in 'Some Tricks of the Trade'.

Our creativity has been stultified. When we were small children, we were masters of 'let's pretend'; we could switch in and out of fantasy at will. Then, as time went by, the concept of 'reality' forced itself more and more into our consciousness, with ideas of right or wrong, truth or lies, and we began to lose our ability to pretend. Pretence has no place in a world of reality.

Primitive cultures have no need of maps; they can see their way from A to B in their mind's eye; they have retained their photographic memories. Because we can write things down, we do not need to retain our photographic memories, so we allow them to fall into disuse. I know adults who say they cannot pretend at all. They maintain that they cannot see pictures in their mind's eye, hear sounds in their mind's ear, or 'pretend' to experience feelings other than those that they are experiencing at this moment, because if something is not real, it has no value. Whether we are imagining something or visualizing our way from A to B, we are making pictures inside our heads, either constructing or recalling them. Whichever we are doing, these pictures are not real: we have created them ourselves. We can create what we want in our heads. We can pretend that we enjoy meetings, that the boss has our best interests at heart, that filling in paperwork is easy, that we understand jargon – anything we like. Try some pretending and see what happens.

If we have to learn about a battle for a history test, there are two things that we can do. We can either sit up all night learning our notes by heart so that we can reproduce them accurately, or we can reread our notes and pretend that we are actually there, seeing what we see: the lie of the land, the colour, the movement, the formations of troops, the generals and their staff, the camp followers, the weather; hearing what we hear: the shouts, the guns, the thundering of hooves, the trumpet calls, the cheers; feeling what we feel (depending on the role we are playing): the excitement, the confusion caused by the noise, the horse beneath us, our companions jostling us; smelling what we smell: the sweat of the horses, the leather, the gunpowder; tasting what we taste: a dry mouth, last night's beer and so on. Which process would be simpler, faster, more fun? And which will produce the better essay?

We are afraid of failure. This must be the most powerful brake upon our abilities: our unconscious mind does not want us to get hurt, and if we failed, we might get hurt. There is a simple remedy for this: if we do not try, we cannot fail. And I wonder what would happen if your unconscious mind became aware that, as far as learning is concerned, passing or failing is not the issue, you would just like to have the fun of acquiring knowledge that might be useful.

We are afraid to change. Maybe we think about the people we know who are successful and decide that we do not want to be like them. Perhaps A is always belittling other people with his command of words; maybe B never seems to enjoy herself; or C does not seem to have many friends. And we certainly do not want to become like them: we would no longer be who we are – we would lose ourselves. Let us pause for a moment and ask ourselves a few serious questions:

- How could success possibly turn us into sarcastic A?
- If we were successful, wouldn't we have more time for fun?
- What would we actually have to do to lose our friends?

A, B and C are themselves, and you are you.

We might wonder how colleagues will react to this change in us, and how it will affect the system to which we belong. We are going to think about identity and systems below.

We do not believe that we deserve to succeed. 'Who do you think you are?' In an effort to discourage children from being selfish, our 'elders and betters' are inclined to imply that we are of no importance, and, if we are of no importance, how could we possibly succeed or be good at anything? Other people can be clever, but not me: there is nothing special about me, I'm just ordinary.

> Once upon a time, in a dark and gloomy gaol, there lived a prisoner. I don't know why he was in prison, and I don't think that he knew either. They had put him into solitary confinement because he was so aggressive, and maybe he was aggressive because he did not understand why he was there, and could not express himself well enough to ask. Some people say that he deserved to be in prison, and maybe he did – I don't know. Nor do I know how long he had been there or how long he had been in solitary confinement. All I do know is that life must have very lonely and very boring for him, but he was used to it because he had forgotten that it could be any different.
>
> Then one day a prison visitor came to see him – at least he said he was a prison visitor. They did not talk much – the prisoner was

not used to talking, and the visitor seemed quite happy to sit in silence – but the prisoner felt that they understood each other, and the silence was companionable and relaxing. And, when the visitor eventually rose to go, he reached into his pocket and took out an envelope, and in that envelope was a tiny seed, which he tipped into the prisoner's hand. 'Take care of this,' he said, 'it is the only one left in the world.' And he was gone, leaving behind a bag that contained a pot, some earth and instructions.

The prisoner planted the seed and put the pot on the high window-sill, where it could get the most light. He watered it when it needed to be watered, and he watched and he waited and waited and waited for a sign of life, until he began to believe that nothing was going to happen at all. Then suddenly, one day, there it was! A tiny little shoot appeared. The prisoner stared at it in wonder: it was really there! He could hardly believe it after all this time. It was so exciting!

For some days he kept his secret hidden deep inside himself – maybe he needed to give himself time to get used to the idea – but then, as the plant grew stronger, he told his gaoler, who took a great interest in it.

And the story spread around the gaol, and people used to come and shout enquiries through the door about how the plant was getting on, until eventually the prison authorities began to allow people into the cell to see for themselves, and our prisoner began to discover how much he enjoyed these visits, and talking about this and that, as well as about his plant.

As the plant grew and grew, the prisoner wondered at its beauty, its balance and symmetry. And then, one day, the prison visitor called again, with another bag.

'I think it's time your plant was repotted,' he said. He turned the pot upside down and tapped it with a trowel.

The prisoner stared in astonishment at the mass of solidly packed roots. 'All that!' he said, 'for such a small plant.'

The visitor smiled. 'All it needed was peace and quiet and time to develop,' he said. And he put the plant carefully into a larger pot, so it could have more space to grow and spread its roots, and more earth to nourish it.

Nobody was bothering to lock the cell door any more and the prisoner was free to come and go as he pleased. And one day the Prison Governor came to admire the plant (which was now just coming into bud), and to ask the prisoner if he would like to work in the prison gardens. I don't know how the prisoner felt about this idea; it must have been strange to think of being outside after all those years; about widening his horizons into an area that he supposedly knew nothing about. All I do know is that he accepted the offer and allowed himself to explore this new world of space, colour, sounds, feeling, taste and smell until he felt completely at home in it and could allow his imagination and ability to develop, until he had created a prison garden such as had never been seen before.

And when the day came for his release, the prisoner went for an interview, which had been arranged for him by the Prison Governor, for the position of gardener at a stately home. As he walked around the gardens, listening to the birds and feasting his eyes upon the beauty of it all, he heard a distant voice: 'It's disgusting, all this wealth. They don't deserve it. This place should be broken up and developed. Why should they have all this, when other people have nothing?'

Our ex-prisoner listened to this and much more as he stood in the formal gardens gazing down, past the fountains, along the great avenue with its folds of ancient trees on either side, to the temple at the bottom and he thought how this landscape had once been just an idea in someone's head, and of how it had grown and developed over the centuries to achieve its present beauty and productiveness. He became aware of how this great estate belonged where it was; of how it had been created for the pleasure and delight of future generations and he mused about all this to the head gardener, who was showing him round.

'We could carry this argument even further,' said his companion, with a smile, 'by asking you whether you deserve this job.'

'Deserve it? Not only do I deserve it, it would also be ungrateful in the extreme to those thousands of people over the centuries who have had a part in the creation of this estate if I were to turn down an offer to enjoy it all, and to add my own contribution to its continued development and success.'

And I will leave you to imagine the pleasure, delight, happiness, harmony and growth that our friend found in his new life.

WHO?

The diagram on page 50 was created by Robert Dilts and Todd Epstein in their development of the work of Gregory

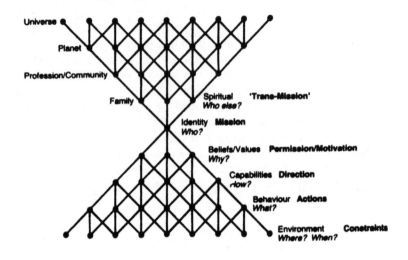

Network of Logical Levels

Bateson, the English scientist whose thinking has provided an intellectual structure for a wide variety of disciplines, from cybernetics to NLP. It shows the relationship between us and our environment, and between us and the universe to which we belong. If we start in the middle of the diagram we can see that our identity is supported by our beliefs and values. I am a learning consultant because I believe that we are all born to learn, because I believe that everyone wants to do well and because I believe that our subjective experience (what goes on inside us) affects everything that we do. Capabilities support these beliefs: I know how to find out what people really want; I know how to rediscover their natural abilities; I know how to discover their subjective experiences. My behaviour creates the capabilities: I give my clients lots of time; I give them my undivided attention; I join them in their models of the world. We find a nice, peaceful place to work, where we won't be interrupted, at a time of day when neither of us is too tired.

This is a very useful diagram for thinking about thinking and for helping us to ask useful questions. For example, 'You say that your boss does not like you. How do you know that?' produces an answer that we can work with, whereas 'Don't be silly; I am sure that he or she does!' is just my belief system opposing yours.

We have already discussed how our 'elders and betters' must be right, because they have had years more experience and thus must know more about the world than we do. We are inclined to believe what they say about us and to build up unhelpful ideas about our identities. 'I am dyslexic; I have a certificate signed by an expert to prove it.' This is an identity statement: 'this is who I am, so there is nothing I can do to change it.' However, dyslexia is about capability and behaviour. People with dyslexia do not yet know how to see letters and words the right way round, and therefore find it difficult to read and reproduce them. We do not say 'I am measlic', we say 'I have measles' – I may be covered in spots at the moment, but measles is not me.

If we get muddled with different logical levels of thought, we can create chaos for ourselves by imagining that because someone once said we were stupid, that is who we are and there is nothing we can do to change it. What did that person actually mean? Did you forget to do what you were told to do? That was a behaviour. Did you fail to answer a question fast enough? That was a capability. Did you break something? That was a behaviour. *The statement had nothing to do with your identity*, and therefore has no effect upon your beliefs about your capabilities.

So who are you really? Stop and think about it. It is a pretty enormous question. You may prefer to choose a metaphor. For example, when I am working on my research, I think of myself as a sea otter. Sea otters live amongst the kelp off the coast of California and as you watch them having a lovely time, you become aware of how they learn through play, through fun, through just being who they are. When I am working with groups, I think of myself as a fountain, producing something that people can see, hear, feel, taste and smell;

something that people can take or leave depending on what they want, while I am provided with an endless source of energy. If you decided to choose a metaphor for yourself, think about why you chose it, what attracted you to it? That is part of who you are. You will find more about using metaphors in 'Mentors, Metaphors and Models'.

The last question I would ask you now is, *are you someone who deserves to succeed?*

WHO ELSE?

From the moment we are born each of us is part of a system that is part of a greater system. Looking at the diagram again, we can see that we are part of the family system (which may include our closest friends). Our family is part of a system of friends, colleagues, neighbours. That system is part of the human race, the human race is part of the planet, and the planet is part of the system that we call the universe.

Who else will be affected if we suddenly become super-learners?

Children become aware of family dynamics at a very early age and, consciously or otherwise, staunch protectors of the family system. It is the only system they know. Change may mean instability, and instability is frightening – we can no longer predict what will happen. How will a small boy feel about what might happen to his illiterate father, whom he worships, if he is made to look a fool by a son who can read and write? If helping her daughter with her maths is the one contribution to the family that a mother feels proud of, what will happen to her mother's role if the daughter can suddenly do maths by herself?

Learning another language may mean behaving in a different way. And behaving in a different way can upset the system. Our parents may not be interested in our revelations about our discoveries at school. If we think that this means that discovering things at school is not contributing to the family system, we may decide to maintain stability by discovering nothing.

Outside the family system, there is the school system. A teacher once told a child I know, who had announced the exciting news that one of his favourite people had just come back from Abu Dhabi, 'There is no such place as Abu Dhabi, Alexander: stop showing off.' Alexander quickly learned not to upset that system, and kept his mouth shut in future. Asking the 'wrong' question can also upset the system if the other person does not know the answer. And how do we know which is the right and which is the wrong question to ask? It may be much safer to give up asking questions altogether.

In order to be able to predict what will happen in any system that we feel a part of, we do our best to maintain the part that we play in it. If someone gives up drinking, what will happen to his long-suffering, supportive, martyred wife when she no longer has that role to fulfil? What will happen to the husband who has always directed all the family affairs when his wife gets a job and becomes financially independent? Do we want to create all this change, unease, and all these identity problems for other people? Or would it be simpler to stay as we are?

You might like to think about who you are as a part of the family system. Then think about who you are in relation to the larger system of friends, colleagues, and the people you spend time with. And what difference would it make to them if you changed? Doing better than our colleagues might make them jealous, which would affect our relationship; it would upset the work system. It may be better to stay as we are.

- If you have always been quiet at work, just getting on with your job and doing what you were told, what would happen if you queried someone's behaviour that struck you as inappropriate?

- If you have always had an answer to everything, what would happen if you said 'I don't know'?

- If you have always been the person who was expected to do something for others, what would happen if you said 'No'?

- Would the company bully turn on someone else if you told him or her to get lost?

- If you have always been predictable, what would happen if people could not rely upon you to do exactly what they expected?

- If you have never voiced your opinion because you had a theory that your opinion was not worth anything, what would happen if you started testing this theory by saying what you think?

- Could other people cope if you changed? And could you cope with the possibility that other people might not be able to cope?

Once upon a time there lived a poor old woman who was so heavy that she could hardly move herself from place to place. She wore dark, flabby clothes that weighed her down, and she looked like a lump of nothing in particular. Now this poor old woman loved her husband and she loved her children, but her husband complained all the time and the children cried all the time, and the poor creature had no friends, because you can't really make friends with a lump of nothing in particular.

One day, when she was hanging out the washing, a wise old gypsy woman appeared carrying a basket of strong hand-made clothes pegs. And she began to talk to our poor lump of nothing in particular. She had a soft, gentle voice and deep, dark eyes in her wise, old face; and the words that she said somehow went straight to our poor friend's heart, and the lump burst into tears.

And when the gypsy asked the poor woman who she was, the woman replied, without even stopping to think, 'I am a bath towel. I am here to absorb all my family's tears, pains, hurts and disappointments.'

The wise gypsy said she thought it was wonderful that this poor creature wanted to wrap up her family in the safety of her love when they were wet and cold and miserable. And she thought how enormous the towel had to be, to be able to wrap up such a big family, and then she gently and kindly explained that when towels get wet, they need to hang out in the sun to dry, to dance in the breeze, to stretch themselves, and she gave the poor lump some special clothes pegs and some lucky heather.

And when the towel was dry and light, and soft and fluffy, our friend was not a poor old woman any more, she was light, supple, flexible, soft, warm, beautiful – as good as new, in bright, swirling clothes, able to enjoy being who she wanted to be while keeping her family warm and dry and safe and comfortable.

I wonder what discoveries you made about yourself and where, when, what, how, and why you do not learn; and how this is affected by who you are and by other people and situations. You might like to make a list.

Some thoughts about values. If you talk to people around the world, you will discover that – whatever race, colour or creed they are – we all share the same top values, such as peace, respect, love, tolerance, co-operation, responsibility, and so on. This discovery has been developed into *'Living Values'*: an education programme for all levels. As you will see from the diagram on page 50, values are at the same level as beliefs, supporting our identity and affecting everything beneath them.

The schools that have adopted *'Living Values'* have discovered that they become a way of life. And, not surprisingly, academic achievement soars – because most of the reasons for Not Learning no longer exist, and because people are now free to be who they are. Schoolchildren in particular have a need to belong; and, if everyone has adopted a certain value for a week/a month/a term, the value provides the basis for belonging.

Having seen a school where everyone knows and looks out for each other, I found myself bewildered and disorientated in a school where people didn't even say 'good morning' to each other. You can find out more about *'Living Values'* from their website (see Useful Addresses).

The 'Living Values' programme won the USA Teacher's Choice award in 2001.

Pause for Thought:
What Do You Want?

We have thought about how we do peculiar things to stop us from feeling bad, and have realized that bad feelings are what we want to get away from, consciously or unconsciously. Now the question is: what do I want to do instead? What would be a satisfying and fulfilling way for me to feel good? If you were a travel agent and I asked you to arrange a holiday for me, you would ask me where I wanted to go. If I told you only that I did not want to be cold and I did not want to be by the sea, I could hardly blame *you* if I found myself in the middle of the desert on a camel, with nothing but party clothes in my luggage, having expected to find myself in a luxury hotel.

So 'What do you want?' and 'What will that give you?' which is another way of asking 'Why do you want that?'

There are no right or wrong answers; there are just *your* answers. The diagram opposite shows an imaginary series of outcomes. Start at the bottom and work your way upwards. My students call this a Christmas Tree.

You can continue way up into the spiritual level if you like. The object of this exercise is to find out whether you really want what you think you want, and to discover what is stopping you from being who you really are. In other words, why do you not already have what you want? In the example it seems that a lack of self-confidence is the obstacle. If you have simply never had the chance to go to the moon, then nothing is stopping you. However, if you believe that you are too

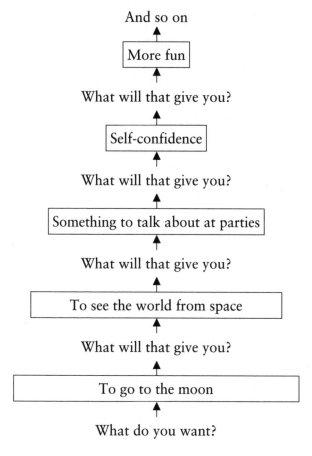

And so on

▲

| More fun |

▲

What will that give you?

▲

| Self-confidence |

▲

What will that give you?

▲

| Something to talk about at parties |

▲

What will that give you?

▲

| To see the world from space |

▲

What will that give you?

▲

| To go to the moon |

▲

What do you want?

Christmas Tree

frightened to do it, ask yourself what is stopping you from having confidence in yourself? And what would happen if you had confidence in yourself?

Now that you know what you want, the next question is: Do you deserve it? Or are all the bad things that people may have said about you really true? When I was a teenager, my father decided for some reason that I was 'discontented', and lectured me about it endlessly. Then, when my younger brother became a teenager and was going through all the things that teenagers go through, father started all over again:

not only was I discontented, I had now succeeded in infecting my brother with this anti-social disease – it was all my fault again. Fortunately, I had decided years earlier that whatever other people might say, I was not *that* bad, so father's diatribe, although irritating, did not cut me to the quick, as it might have done.

During a workshop with John Grinder our homework one evening was to remember all the old family sayings that had worked themselves deep into our unconscious minds and could now hold us back. Some interesting ones came up:

- Who do you think you are?
- Stop giving yourself airs.
- 'I want' doesn't get.
- Who's going to pay any attention to you?
- He's got ideas above his station.
- You don't deserve it.
- No pain, no gain.
- What makes you think you are important?
- Think of yourself last.
- She thinks she's the bee's knees.

One of my favourite broadcasters, Rabbi Lionel Blue, turned my world upside down by saying " 'Love thy neighbour as thyself' means 'as much as thyself', so, if you do not love yourself, you are of no use whatever to your neighbour." This was not how I had been taught to interpret it, and of course it makes infinitely more sense than allowing everyone else to run steamrollers over us.

A DREAM BEYOND THE DREAM

The nineteenth century German playwright Georg Büchner tells a story about the child who cried for the moon and when she got it, she found that it was nothing but a lump of rotting cheese. The Chinese say that when we finish our house, we die, and John Grinder says 'Always keep a dream beyond your dream' so that when you have reached your dream, you have something else to move on to, otherwise, what will you do when you have nothing else to do? Fear of success is often a fear of having nothing to look forward to: I've achieved it; I've made it, now where on earth do I go from here? I keep asking 'What will that give you?' when I am working with outcomes, to clarify the dream beyond the dream. Your outcomes are your thoughts here and now; you can change them whenever and however you want as new and even more exciting ideas come to you.

Come to Your Senses!

Learning, as we have seen, is two processes: we take information in through one or more of our five senses, and we reproduce that information when required. From all the work done under hypnosis in order to recall past events, it would appear that the information goes in whether or not we are consciously aware of it. All we have to do now is to streamline our filing and cross-referencing systems in order to be able to retrieve what we need when we want it.

It is becoming easier and easier to track books down. In the old days we needed to know the title, the author and the publisher; now, if I want to find a book I heard about weeks ago, and I have no idea who wrote it, but I know that it was about a bridge, a bookseller can produce a list of every book in print with the word 'bridge' in the title, which I can look through until I recognize the one I want. This is a very useful cross-referencing system, but booksellers' computers have only words and numbers, whereas we have all five senses, which makes things much simpler for us. We are now going to think about our five senses: about how and where we code the information they receive, and how we retrieve it when we want it.

The exercises in this section are designed to develop learning systems that we may have forgotten to use and to enhance those we use a lot. The trick is to allow the discoveries that you make to generalize across every aspect of your life. For example, if you are enhancing your auditory abilities in order to remember names better, you can use the same strategies for remembering what somebody told you yesterday, or who said what at a meeting.

NB: The object of all the experiments is to allow people to discover for themselves just how clever they are, by starting with something easy and increasing the difficulty according to how well-developed each system is: giving people a hard time will just make them think they cannot do it, when of course they can, although they may not be aware of it. Some people will be better at the visual exercises, some at the auditory, and some at the kinaesthetic ones, depending on which they use most.

LEARNING THROUGH OUR EYES

Seeing is believing?

Look at the picture below. Does it show an old woman, or a young woman?

In fact, there are two women in this picture; some people will see one, and some will see the other. When you point out that there are two women, some people can see the second one easily and some cannot see her at all. The young woman is looking away over her left shoulder. You can see her right ear, her jawline, the ribbon round her neck, the tip of her nose and her right eyelashes. You can see the old woman's right profile, with her chin tucked down between the furs wrapped round her raised shoulders.

We have different perceptions of the world. People will argue passionately about what is in the picture and, even when they know there are two women, they will become exasperated when someone else still cannot see the woman that they see. There is so much information out there in the world that we only take in at a conscious level what we want, or think that we need, to see. For example, I have an excellent filter system when it comes to dust: I do not see it at all. In an exercise John Grinder suggested that we take on a quality that we thought we would like to have, to discover what would happen if we had it. I chose attention to detail, because I wanted to be able to appreciate the finer points of craftsmanship and I discovered to my horror that I was wandering around the beautiful room noticing chips on the fireplace, peeling wallpaper and bits missing from the mouldings – none of which I wanted to see at all.

As we discovered earlier, with Necker's cube, the brain needs to make sense of the information it receives and so, if it has insufficient information, it will fill in the gaps. When my cousin started to see unusual things because of a brain tumour, she decided that they were dogs; she knew that they were hallucinations, but enjoyed the idea of having extra dogs about the house. The illustration on page 63 is from *Mind Skills* by David Lewis. What is it? Allow yourself fifteen seconds, and then read on.

Some people see a head and shoulders, some people see a baby; their minds are joining different dots, filling in different blanks. What do you see? It is, in fact, a man on a horse and once you know that, you can fill in the blanks quite easily.

What does this figure show?

Seeing what is there

> What is this life, if full of care,
> We have no time to stand and stare?
>
> William Henry Davies (1871–1940)

In our society there seems to be something shockingly immoral about standing and staring. We are expected to be busy, rushing from pillar to post all day. If someone catches us staring at the swans on the river, we hastily explain that we are on our way somewhere and have paused only for a moment because we realized we were early, or we are waiting for someone – anything rather than admit that we are 'wasting' time, just enjoying looking at something.

How are we supposed to learn to see things properly if we never give ourselves time to look? How can we ever get to enjoy using our eyes if we never have the time to spare? How can we learn to appreciate a landscape, a building, a work of art if we never pause in front of it? As your fairy godmother, my present to you would be time. Time to enjoy everything that comes to you through your five senses, starting with your eyes. Time to discover the world outside ourselves.

Try watching television with the sound turned down to see how much information you can pick up without any words or mood-setting music. There is endless information to be gained just from watching.

Here is a game that children enjoy too.

You are from outer space on a visit to Earth, and in contact with your space ship by radio. Your job is to describe things that you find to the Earth Expert in the ship, so that he or she can guess what they are. This is your first visit to Earth, so you know nothing about our curious customs. For example, your description might be 'It is a cold shiny object, heavy for its size and about as long as my hand. It starts long and thin – as wide as my middle finger – then it gets narrower. The thin part is about a third longer than my middle finger; then it spreads out into a depressed circle at the other end. I can see my face upside down in the circle.' You continue with your description until the Earth Expert has decided that you are describing a soup spoon.

The Earth Visitor is using his or her observation skills, while the Earth Expert is using visual construct skills.

Visual memory

Visual memory is almost perfect – if we know where to look. I lost my purse one day, searched high and low, failed to find it and eventually set off without it. Relaxed, in the car, I did the first sensible thing in my search: I flashed my eyes up to my left, where I keep my visual memories, and there I saw myself putting lots of rubbish I had collected from my car into the bin. Unable to believe that I could have thrown out my purse, I stepped into the picture, and felt the weight of the purse under the rest of the rubbish; back I went, and there it was!

To get the best use from our visual memory, we need to know where in our brain we file our pictures. Ask people questions that involve visual memory and you will notice that their eyes will flash up – generally to the left, with right-handed people – in order to find the image they have stored.

Here are some questions you can use to test this theory on your friends. If their eyes do not move, the questions are too easy, so try something that will make them really search in their memories. These eye movements are very fast, so have each question in your head so that you can watch while you ask it; if you read the question to them and then look, you will miss the movement. As you think about the answers to these questions for yourself, you will become aware of how you are checking on your internal pictures.

- What colour is your front door?
- What shape is Australia?
- What did Charlie Chaplin look like?
- Remember a beautiful sunset.
- What was the first film you ever saw?
- What was your best friend wearing last time you saw him or her?
- What colour was the front door of your first school?
- Describe the place you live in from the outside

Because I do not know your friends, these questions are not particularly interesting; you will be able to think up some much better ones, like the colour of so-and-so's eyes. The important thing to remember is that we all have different filing systems. There is no 'right' or 'wrong' place to keep remembered images; we just need to know where they are.

Some people know that they make internal pictures. Some people will swear that they never do and if you ask them how they recognize people, they will tell you that they just do. These are the interesting ones. Ask them to describe a spiral staircase without using their hands, and see what happens – where do their eyes go and what sort of language do they use? Listen for expressions like:

- Let me see.
- It looks ...
- In my view ...

- The way I see it.
- Let's get this into perspective.
- If we focus on ...
- I can't see the connection.
- any other visual phrases.

If you insist upon pointing out that they are using internal pictures, do it very gently – a lot of people do not like having their theories disproved.

Visual memory is particularly good at enabling us to reproduce precise things like charts and diagrams. In *Make the Most of Your Mind* Tony Buzan teaches us how to create mind maps instead of writing boring notes, so that our visual memories can see the colours and the shapes and reproduce all the information without any difficulty. We use visual memory for all sorts of things including remembering how to get to places or where we left the car, for noticing what has changed about something or someone. We can also use it to remember how something works, if we saw the moving parts, or how somebody did something; to remember where we last saw something that we have lost, or to remember a scene, a meeting or an argument so that we can replay it in our heads if we need a better understanding of what happened. People who have developed their photographic memories can reproduce whole pages of a book, and many of us can remember where we saw something in a book or a newspaper when we need to find it again in a hurry; for example, at the top of a right-hand page, somewhere towards the end.

You can now start becoming aware of where, when and how you are using your visual memory most effectively, and noticing how your friends and family are using theirs by the way their eyes move, by the words that they use and by asking them. People talk much faster when they are in visual mode because their information is coming in at such speed. Other people may have useful strategies that you had not thought of: if you think you have a rotten memory for faces or names, ask someone who has a good one how they do it, and then use their strategy. The great advantage of visual memory is that it is fast. It is a thousand times quicker to see an internal picture than it is to repeat remembered words; think how long it took to describe simple objects to the Earth Expert in the last game.

Get one or more friends to pose, as if for a photograph. Allow your brain to take an internal picture of them – the exposure can be as long or as short as you like. Then close your eyes and ask them to change one thing each: they may want to move a foot or a hand – something reasonably obvious the first time; then open your eyes and tell them what has changed.

When you have successfully done this, you can become aware of just how much information you had to process in order to get it right. You can ask yourself how you did it. How did you find the memory of what the people looked like before they moved? How did you compare that memory to the new poses? Did you have the two pictures side by side, to compare and contrast, or did you superimpose one picture upon another to show up the differences? Or did you do something else? And how did you do whatever you did? This is your strategy for visual memory, which you can use whenever you need it.

If you think that you do not know the answers to these questions, what would the answers be if you did know? In other words, guess! The answer that comes off the top of your head will be the answer from your unconscious mind; and your unconscious mind knows. After you have discovered what your strategy is, you can repeat the experiment to enhance your visual memory, asking your friends to make the task gradually more and more difficult for you, until eventually the differences become very small, like taking off earrings, or doing up a button. I remember posing for Phyllis. The only change I made was to move my name badge from the left to the right. Phyllis put her hand up to her name badge and said, 'I don't know.' Her unconscious was showing her.

On my way to sleep, when I am warm, comfortable and relaxed, I like to remember or create scenes for a story or just for fun. I may be remembering a favourite garden, a favourite walk, a favourite house or a favourite room, and I like to bring back the proportions, the shapes, the colours, the light, the shade, the movement. Then, maybe, I will change things around a bit, add things, take things away – just for fun. A left-handed friend of mine keeps all his happy memories above him and to the right, from where he can pull them down and enjoy them again. He describes himself as a 'great memory-laner'.

Try describing one friend to another, and see how long it takes for the other person to recognize who you are talking about.

These are just a few suggestions to fire your imagination. I do not know which musician said 'I never practise; I play!', and the more we play around with our visual memories, the better they will get. Our brains learn at amazing speed, and once your brain realizes that visual memory is what you want, it will provide it.

LEARNING THROUGH OUR EARS

A sympathy with sounds

> There is in souls a sympathy with sounds;
> And as the mind is pitch'd the ear is pleased
> With melting airs, or martial, brisk or grave:
> Some chord in unison with what we hear
> Is touch'd within us, and the heart replies.
> William Cowper (1731–1800)

Sounds transmit information to our brains, and we interpret new information according to the information that we already have. As with our eyes, we filter out what we do not need. People who live in towns are probably unaware of the constant sound of traffic. If I am concentrating on something, I am not consciously aware of the radio playing in the background or the fire crackling in the hearth – they are not necessary to what I am doing now, although they will be recorded in my unconscious. We need to know where to find the file for auditory memory; you probably keep yours below your visual memory. Ask people to remember a sound, and they are likely to look towards one ear.

- When did you last hear church bells?
- What does a police siren sound like?
- What does your alarm clock sound like?
- What are the first four notes of Beethoven's Fifth Symphony?
- Remember the sound of waves crashing on the rocks.
- Remember the sound of heavy rain.
- Remember the last telephone conversation you had.
- Describe Nelson Mandela's voice.

These are some questions you can ask your friends and family. Where did your eyes go as you were recalling the sounds? Once again, if they did not move, my questions were too easy: find yourself some more difficult sounds to remember – maybe something you heard longer ago or something you have heard only once.

A lot of the information that comes into our brains by way of sound will be words. When we are recalling words, we are more likely to remember the way they were delivered than the words themselves, because words on their own make up less than 10 per cent of our communication. It's not what we say, it is how we say it that is important. What is the sound of those words? Is the pitch high or low? Is the sound loud or soft? What is the tone like? What is the rhythm? Which words are being stressed? Where are the pauses? There is a mass of information to interpret and code.

Sound is vibration. Don Campbell, the Director of the Institute for Music, Health and Education in Boulder, Colorado, tells us that marine biologists have known for years that a fish's body is an extension of its ears, and he wonders when human biologists will realize that the same thing applies to us.

We absorb sound through our whole bodies, and rhythm affects our entire being.

Try this experiment – you will need some baroque music (by composers from the first half of the eighteenth century, like Albinoni, Bach, Corelli, Handel, Teleman and Vivaldi) and some heavy rock, like Led Zeppelin. You will also need someone to help you.

1. Settle yourself down comfortably and listen to some baroque music for about five minutes. Then get someone to test your arm strength: hold your stronger arm out to one side at a right angle to your body. The tester puts a hand on your wrist and, while you resist, gently presses your arm downwards. Ask the tester to give you a score from 1 to 10.

2. Repeat the experiment, this time listening to the heavy rock music and compare your scores.

I tried this experiment with a friend, who insisted that I test both his arms after the baroque music to prove that he could get 10 out of 10 for his left arm as well. When he discovered that he was so weak after the heavy rock music that he could hardly resist at all, he was furious and produced every excuse you can imagine. He is probably still trying to convince himself that I cheated in some fiendish way.

A friend's son was having trouble with his mathematics homework. Although she did not really believe the stories I had told her, Susan put a tape of baroque music into her son's personal stereo to see what would happen: he raced through his homework in no time at all. Some sounds strengthen us, and some sounds weaken us. Baroque music was written to free the soul from earthly matters, with its perfect symmetry and harmony. I play it in my workshops, when I am with clients and when I am slaving away over the word processor.

Sound vibrates our skulls, and this massages and stimulates our brains. Professor Alfred Tomatis, who has done some fascinating work with sound, tells the story of how he was summoned to a monastery in France where the monks appeared to be dying; I suspect he was called in as a last resort after every other specialist had been tried. What he wanted to know was what had changed in the monastery routine before the monks became ill. He discovered that the new abbot had decided that the time spent in chanting could be used more productively, so chanting had been stopped, and the monks, whose brains had been massaged by chant for several hours a day for years and years, suddenly had no stimulation. Without stimulation, the brain dies, and if the brain dies, the body dies. Tomatis insisted that chanting be restored and all the monks recovered. If you are tired or depressed, sing!

Don Campbell maintains that the only reason why people sing out of tune is because someone sang out of tune to them when they were young. He demonstrates this by finding someone who claims that he or she cannot sing in tune. He puts his right hand on their left cheek, and their right hand on his left cheek. Then he sings a note, and the other person will sing either the same note or a note in harmony with Don. If that does not work, he does it cheek to cheek. I have never known this experiment to fail.

I have always loved the sound of African singing and never knew why until one day when we were singing with Titos Sompa: he was singing phrases and we were repeating them. Suddenly I became aware that we sounded like Africans. Then I remembered Don: we were not trying to sing the same note as Titos, we were just resonating with him, simply singing what we felt would be in harmony with him, and the result was beautiful.

Listening

Listening is not taught at school and some people never really seem to learn to do it at all. This may be because they have so much internal dialogue going on that it is drowning out the external sound. It may be because they have run a program since babyhood whereby talking makes them feel better. It may be because they are consciously or unconsciously afraid that the other person is going to be able to outwit them with

words. Learning through listening is simply about allowing
ourselves to let go: about giving ourselves permission to let go
of old rubbish and allowing information to flow in. Information is simply information. Our brains are more than capable
of sorting it as it comes in, and when it is all there, we can
accept or reject what we will. Some people are afraid that if
they do not interrupt to ask a question *now*, they will forget
whatever it was that they wanted to ask. If we make an internal picture of all the information as it comes in, we will still be
aware of the gaps in our picture when the person has finished
talking; and by that time we will probably have been given
enough additional information to fill in the gap for ourselves.

My headmistress used to read to us, and she liked us to bring
something to do at the same time, like knitting or needlework.
This distracted our conscious minds, leaving the unconscious
free to absorb the whole story. A story has a beginning, a
middle and an end, and a good story is carefully constructed so
that every part is important; if we concentrate on picking holes
in one part of it, we are going to miss some of the rest.

When my students are learning to get their tongues round a
new language, they listen to short phrases and then repeat
them. While they are listening they will be doing something
else, like juggling or skipping – anything to distract the conscious mind. They repeat what they hear, not what they think
they ought to have heard. The result is that their accents are
superb, because the conscious mind is too busy to keep
reminding them that they are going to get it wrong.

Try listening to the same piece of music in different ways:

- with your head, analysing it;
- with your heart, enjoying the emotion it stirs;
- with your stomach, experiencing the rhythm and vibration.

What differences do you experience inside you when you do
this? What pictures do you see in your mind's eye? What
sounds do you hear in your mind's ear? What different sensations do you feel, and where do you feel them? What happens
if you just listen to the music and allow your eyes to move

with the notes? How do they move as the music moves? The way that they move, if you allow them to, will show you how you record different sounds and rhythms in your brain.

Spend some time with your eyes closed, just enjoying the pleasure of listening to the sounds all around you, and your own heartbeat and breathing.

Words mean different things to different people. To make sure that we have understood the message, it is useful to feed back to the speaker what we think they have just said. Josephine was telling me about her work, and how her company provided resources to help small businesses. Jim came to join us and I relayed to him what I had just learned from Josephine. She was horrified when I told Jim that her company provided money to help small businesses. To me, 'resources' meant 'money'; that was how I filed it and I was not even aware that I had changed the words. There was no question of Josephine's company providing money: 'resources' meant practical help. This was a valuable lesson. Now if I am not sure what someone means by a certain word or phrase, I ask.

Experiment with feeding back to people what you think they have just said. People love talking, especially on a favourite subject. It will be such a pleasure for them to have someone who is really listening to them for a change. It can also be a great help to people to realize how what they say is received when they are discussing something close to their hearts; they can discover whether they are getting their message across as effectively as they would like.

As you do this, you will gradually become aware of how you are doing it, of how you are remembering what was said. Are you just recalling the words and replaying the tape in your mind? Are you putting the words into pictures and feeding back from the pictures? Are you checking the words out with your feelings? Or are you doing something completely different? Alternatively are you doing lots of different things? And if you are, which work best? And how are you doing whatever it is that you do?

The next experiment is one of Judith DeLozier's and it is a lot of fun. You will need two other people.

C sits with his or her eyes closed, just listening. The other two are going to make the same sound: it may be a clap, a flick of the fingers – whatever they choose. Let us imagine they have chosen to clap. A claps once, and says 'A'; B claps once and says 'B'. They repeat this until C can tell the difference between the sounds. When C is confident about being able to tell the difference, A and B can stop saying who is clapping and allow C to guess.

The trick here is for A and B to enforce every right guess by saying 'yes'. If C makes a mistake, the person who has been misheard simply claps again, saying his or her name, so that C can reset his or her memory without hearing demoralizing words like 'no' or 'wrong'.

Once again, when you have discovered that you can do this, you can ask yourself how you did it. How did you produce memories of two different sounds? How did you compare and contrast the sound you had just heard with those auditory memories? How did you decide which sound was which?

All these experiments are designed for you discover which strategy works best for you: what do *you* do in order to guess correctly? What is the difference that makes the difference between a strategy that works and one that doesn't? It is fun to discover other people's strategies and to try them out. Invent some more games for yourself and your family to enhance your listening skills.

Now that you are beginning to become more consciously aware of the extraordinary skills that you have been using unconsciously all this time, you may be wondering what other surprise resources you have at your disposal. As you read on, you will find more experiments to enhance your listening skills at the same time as becoming aware of your kinaesthetic skills: the way you use your body to pick up messages from the world around you.

You can now reward yourself with some self indulgence.

Put on some nice, soothing music, preferably baroque or Mozart. Take the telephone off the hook and settle yourself somewhere deliciously warm and comfortable, knowing that you can readjust your position whenever your body suggests it. Close your eyes and allow the music to transport you to wherever you would like to go.

And maybe your conscious mind might find relaxation a little dull, so you might like to give it permission to go off and do something completely different, knowing that it can come back and join you whenever you need it. You might like to allow those conscious thoughts to float up and away in balloons while you keep the strings tied to your left big toe, or you might like to wrap them in a velvet bag and put them somewhere safe for the time being. I don't know what your conscious mind would like best; all I do know is that you and your conscious mind will have the answers to these questions.

You may choose to go to the mountains; you may choose to go to the sea; you may choose a favourite walk; you may choose to invent somewhere special for yourself. I don't know where you will choose to go or what you will choose to do, because this is your private, special time for *you* to spend as long as you like in your favourite place, doing your favourite things.

And I wonder what you will see in your favourite place; what shapes, forms, colours, contours, perspectives, movements, lights, shadows, different shades of different colours, grand designs, fine details, balance, symmetry, harmony, reflections. I don't know what you will see.

And I wonder what you will hear in your favourite place; close sounds, distant sounds, high sounds, low sounds, long sounds, short sounds, sounds that belong to your favourite place, expected sounds, unexpected sounds, harmonious sounds, dissonant sounds, warm sounds, cold sounds. I don't know what you will hear.

And I wonder whether hearing new sounds will show you new sights, and whether seeing new sights will point you towards new sounds, and whether you will be interested and surprised by all that there is to see and to hear as you move around in your favourite place, turning your head this way and that to absorb all that is old and familiar and all that is new and interesting.

And I wonder if there is anything that you would like to change to make your favourite place even more special and personal to you; if there are any sights and sounds that you would like to add or take away or alter in any way.

And I know that you know that you can do anything that you want in your mind's eye, and anything that you want in your mind's ear.

And I wonder when you will begin to become aware of feelings, tastes and smells, as you enjoy yourself in your favourite place for as long as you like, knowing that when you choose to come back to the here and now, you will feel refreshed and relaxed, and surprised and pleased about everything that you have experienced and created.

My students do variations of this at the beginning of every day for fun, for relaxation and for enhancing their five senses.

LEARNING THROUGH OUR FEELINGS

Trust your body

The best way to learn through your body is to be in it consciously. Some of us are there most of the time, and some of us seem to forget that we have bodies at all and live entirely in our heads. We ignore aches and pains and tensions, either by pretending they are not there or by taking an aspirin; we do not stop to wonder what it is all about. Simply being aware of tension, and acknowledging it, will allow the body to readjust to a more comfortable position.

In *The Inner Game of Tennis* Timothy Gallwey tells us that the standard of tennis in Britain soars after Wimbledon; tennis players have probably spent hours watching the experts on television and their bodies have acquired a lot of new information. If someone tells Gallwey that they cannot do something, he asks them to show him how an expert would do it. In *The Inner Game of Skiing* he tells us how he asked one woman to demonstrate how a famous skier would tackle a difficult slope that she was afraid to take on: off she went, got triumphantly to the bottom and said, 'That's how he'd do it but, of course, I couldn't do that.'

Our bodies know what they are doing; after all, they look after us twenty-four hours a day, although they get precious little thanks for it. Try saying 'hello' and 'thank you' to your body in a friendly, appreciative tone, as though you really mean it, *now*, and see how pleased and surprised it is.

Here is an experiment devised by John Whitmore. You will need someone to help you.

Hold your arm out to your side at right angles to your body (as you did with the music experiment), and get your partner to try to push it down gently, while you resist. Be aware of which muscles you are using in order to resist.

Now imagine that your arm is steel, oak or anything you like that cannot bend, which is projecting right through you and into the nearest wall; it may take a moment or two to get yourself into this state. When you are ready, your partner can try to press your arm down again. This time you will provide no resistance, you will just maintain whatever image you have chosen for your arm. You will find you are much stronger.

As John Whitmore says, 'Why use your back, neck and jaw muscles, just to keep your arm straight? What a waste of energy!'

We have seen how taking on somebody else's physiology can change our model of reality. A student of mine was having trouble with his boss and I suggested that he 'become' his boss to discover what was going on inside him. He managed to do it for a fraction of a second – it was such a horrible experience that he did not want to stay there. He came back to himself understanding just why his boss was so awful – physiology like that made him feel terrible.

Try another experiment.

Think about something that really depresses you, and then walk around briskly with your head up, looking up at the ceiling, the rooftops, the treetops, whatever you can see that is higher than you. Try to maintain all those depressing thoughts as you walk around. You will find that you cannot. Feelings are filed *down*, probably towards the hand you write with, and with your eyes up, you cannot access bad feelings effectively.

If you have a friend who is feeling depressed, try the patent Beaver remedy and take him or her out kite-flying.

This is Joseph O'Connor's experiment.

1 Throw a ball up into the air – not too high – and catch it. Establish a comfortable rhythm of throwing and catching, and then try closing your eyes when the ball reaches the top of its flight; you will find that your body knows how to catch it even though you cannot see it.

2 Throw the ball in an arc from hand to hand (with the top of the arc just above your head). Again, establish a comfortable rhythm, then close your eyes when the ball reaches the top of the arc. Once again, you will discover that you do not need to see the ball in order to be able to catch it.

How did you manage to catch the ball with your eyes shut? What did you do? Where did you put your attention? What did you feel and where did you feel it? Being aware of what you did and how you did it means that you and your body are getting to know each other again.

As a dancer Judith DeLozier is an endless source of ideas for getting information into and from our bodies, and here is another of her experiments.

Find a stick – a walking stick will be fine – put on a blindfold and with a friend to act as your Guardian Angel, go out and explore without the use of your eyes, knowing that your Guardian Angel is there to keep you safe.

I did this with Tere and she, being a city girl, stayed close to the buildings, whereas when it was my turn, I set off across country. Each of us chose territory where we felt most comfortable, and each thought the other was crazy to wander around blindfolded in such a dangerous area.

Still blindfolded, try following sounds.

I remember dancing after Loren at tremendous speed, up and down hills, in and out of trees, singing 'Ninety-nine bottles of beer on the wall', and the only thing that suffered was my ability to count backwards from ninety-nine.

Try dancing blindfolded with a partner, touching only the tips of each other's fingers; this gives a wonderful awareness of space and movement.

Here is the kinaesthetic version of the visual and auditory experiments you tried earlier with A, B and C.

C is blindfolded. A and B touch C on the same spot, saying who they are, until C can tell the difference.

There are endless variations: A and B can pass their hands across C's face, without touching it, or they can sit down beside C. What other ideas can you come up with?
The next experiment is John Grinder's idea.

Blindfolded, throw your keys, or some other object that you carry around most of the time, some distance away from you. Someone spins you round. Then go and find whatever it is.

These experiments are all extensions of Gregory Bateson's questions about the boundaries of self in a system: where does self end, and something else begin? Does a blind person end at his or her fingertips? Or at the end of the stick? Or half way down the stick?
How did you do all these things? How did you know when there was an obstacle in your way without touching it? Were you bouncing sounds off obstacles like a bat? Did you feel the air thickening as you approached an obstacle? How did you know which way to turn? How did you know when it was

safe to take a step when you did not have a stick to guide you? What were you doing inside yourself in order to know all these things? Where were you placing your attention?

Try some T'ai Chi.

Stand face to face and palm to palm with a partner; your hands are not touching – they are just close enough so that you can feel each other's warmth and energy. Person A moves their hands (slowly to start with), and person B follows the movement. After a while, change over so B leads the movement and A follows. Then neither of you leads, and you will find that the dance continues because each of you knows what to do. You can bring in more movement whenever you want, such as stepping slowly forwards or backwards, and increasing the speed as your awareness heightens.

I remember doing this along the branch of a tree with a colleague while discussing an exercise that we had to set up. Again, where do the boundaries of self end?

Experimenting with other models

How do you breathe? Which part of your body moves most when you take in air? Is it your stomach? Your rib cage? The upper part of your chest? People in different modes breathe in different ways. In visual mode, everything seems to have an upward direction, the breathing will be in the upper chest, the voice may get higher; maybe the person is trying to get closer to the pictures up in their visual field. In auditory mode the rib cage will be expanding and contracting towards and away from the sounds. In kinaesthetic mode the breathing will be in the stomach, lowering the centre of gravity and putting the person in touch with their feelings; kinaesthetic people have a slow, quiet rhythm, giving themselves plenty of time to check out information with their bodies. Colin and I drive each other mad when we are discussing business: I have to keep up with my rapidly changing pictures while he has to check everything out with his stomach.

Richard, who is a tracker, taught us to watch people's feet as they walk along. If their feet are pointing straight ahead, they are in visual mode; if one foot turns out, they are listening in that direction; if both feet are slightly turned out, they are in auditory mode; and if the feet are really turned out, they are in kinaesthetic mode.

- What would happen if you changed your breathing for a while to experiment with a different model of the world, to see what it has to offer? What extra information would you pick up? What information, if any, would you lose?

- What would happen if you changed the way you walk by changing the direction in which your feet point? If you are usually visual, try walking like a dancer, with your feet turned out, really in touch with the ground. The actress, Beryl Reid says that once she has got the shoes right, she has got the character right.

These changes may feel strange, and you may decide that you do not like them. In that case you can ask yourself what it is that you do not like. Is it really unpleasant or is it just something unknown? We are rather inclined to shy away from unknown experiences because they are strange, without stopping to ask ourselves either whether they might have any useful information for us or whether this strange feeling might be something worth trying to see what happens. During a seminar with John Grinder, when we were modelling the healer Finnbar Nolan, I suddenly found myself taking great gulps of air. From that moment on, my breathing changed from fast, high, visual mode (which probably was not providing me with enough oxygen anyway) down into much slower, deeper expansion of the rib cage and stomach; this opened up whole new worlds of awareness for me. Thérèse Berthérat describes the same experience in *The Body Has Its Reasons*, a wonderful book of what she calls 'anti-exercises and self-awareness'.

Titos teaches us African dance. Judy was brought up with Western dance in which she was taught to count the steps as she danced. One day she asked Titos how far she had to count in order to know when to move from one part of the dance to the next. He looked at her as though she were an idiot child and said, 'But the drums tell you.' These two dancers both use a combination of sound and rhythm to know the right moment, and yet each has a different model of the world.

Kinaesthetic memory

Our muscles have memory. They know how it feels to ride a bicycle, to run for a bus, to jump into a swimming pool. They also remember how to spell. We use our kinaesthetic memory all the time. Whenever we allow our thoughts about someone or something to make us feel bad, and whenever we are bringing back the pleasures of happy memories, our bodies are responding to everything that those memories conjure up.

Think about an argument that you had with someone recently, and experience what happens inside your body.

Then shake off those feelings because you no longer need those memories. Now think about the last time you were really enjoying yourself. Step right back into the scene and relive it, appreciating all the sensations you are experiencing throughout your body, as you enjoy yourself again.

Then you can ask yourself how you did both these things. Did you see a picture first, and did this picture bring the feelings with it? Did you hear sounds first? How did you conjure up your kinaesthetic memory? What did you do to find those memories? Once you know that, your kinaesthetic memory is available to you whenever you need it.

When clients come to me with broken bones, we do exercises in their imaginations; the leg may be in plaster but in its imagination it is running, jumping, walking – doing whatever its owner likes doing. All the micro-muscles are at work, and when the plaster comes off, the bone is well healed and the muscle wastage almost non-existent.

LEARNING THROUGH TASTE AND SMELL

> ... the smell and the taste of things remain poised a long
> time, like souls, ready to remind us, waiting and hoping
> for their moment ... and bear unfaltering, in the tiny and
> almost impalpable drop of their essence, the vast struc-
> ture of recollection.
>
> Marcel Proust, *Remembrance of Things Past*

When my son Hugo was very young, he caused a great stir on
a visit to an aviary by helping himself to a mouthful of
maggots. I was alerted by shrieks of horror from other scan-
dalized visitors, and poor Hugo was dragged away before the
frailer members of the assembled company passed out. He
was furious – apparently the maggots were delicious.

We have already thought about babies putting everything
in their mouths: the lips and mouth are so sensitive that there
is a mass of information to be had from this piece of research.
Having been deprived of this excellent learning channel at an
early age, on the grounds of hygiene and safety, all that is left
to us is taste and its effect. Smells, too, may well be buried
fairly deeply in the subconscious, but, like tastes, they are
there none the less, and hard at work on your behalf. Try this
experiment.

> Imagine you are holding a lemon. Look at it: its size, its
> shape, its colour, the way it is lying in your hand. Roll it
> around in your hands so that you can feel the shape, and the
> texture of the skin. Roll it against your cheek. Smell it. Now
> imagine that you are cutting it in half: watch the knife
> cutting through it; hear the sound as it cuts through the
> flesh and out the other side; see the juice running; smell the
> freshly running juice; and now pick up one half and sink
> your teeth into it.
>
> What happens to your mouth?

What goes on in your mouth is a good monitor of what
is going on inside you. There is an extraordinary Spanish
surgeon who performs major operations without anaesthetic.
(An image that I will never forget is of one of his patients

chattering away while the surgeon was operating on her leg.) And one thing that this surgeon insists upon is that his patients maintain a high level of saliva. Faced with a particularly terrifying fairground ride, I filled my mouth with saliva and thoroughly enjoyed the experience. Try it the next time your courage is being challenged and see what happens.

Cooks use their sense of taste and smell all the time. Smell is indispensable when shopping for freshness and flavour. It also comes in handy for alerting us when a cake is done, when the oven needs to be turned down for a stew, when the flour has been cooked just long enough for a sauce or – as very often in my case – when something is burning. When my son Mark was about two and a half, the smell of very hot oil brought me out of sleep and down the stairs in seconds: 'Look, Mummy! My cook breakfast! One for you, one for me, one for Daddy and one for my baby!' And there in the frying-pan, over the heat turned up high, were four eggs rapidly blackening round the edges. (Mark had not been deterred by the out-of-the-reach-of-children knobs; he had simply climbed on to a chair to reach them.)

I remember a workshop where I said casually, 'When I rule the world, cookery and chemistry will be taught together'. There was an explosion from the back: 'I have never heard anything so ridiculous in my life. I was enjoying your presentation ... and then you go and make a stupid remark like that. I am a chemist. And I can assure you that chemistry has nothing whatever to do with cookery.' I apologized, saying that I was just a cook, and, for me, cooking had everything to do with chemistry. What I had done (unintentionally) was to equate my behaviour when cooking with his identity as a chemist; the result: instant rejection. NLP presupposes that the meaning of the communication is the response that you get; my communication did not work.

Tastes and smells can transport us, consciously or unconsciously, straight back to childhood. This may be to an open, curious, learning state, or it may be to a state where we feel small and vulnerable and in urgent need of protecting ourselves by closing all our learning channels.

If you listen, you will hear how people are unconsciously using taste and smell in their calculations. These expressions come from basic awareness:

- It smells fishy.
- I smell a rat.
- It leaves a nasty taste in your mouth.
- It stinks.
- It makes you want to spit.

'Flair' comes from the French for 'a sense of smell', which also means 'intuition', and the French tap their noses as they use it, in the same way that we may tap ours when we are suspicious of someone. And what about 'Good Taste'?

Taste and smell are always available to us as a way of remembering. As you discovered with the lemon, it is possible to be affected by things that are not there. So have fun! Smell what you want to smell and taste what you want to taste in your imagination.

GETTING YOUR ACT TOGETHER

Although I have divided our learning equipment into five different senses, the senses are, of course, all interconnected, sometimes in unexpected ways. For example, I am delighted when I can smell things that I see on television, curious when people tell me that they were listening to clapping in a particular language, and fascinated when someone asks: 'Do you want to see the noise?' When I was at school, the ethos was to get us out of our bodies and into our heads. If we were not extremely auditory, we did not survive the talk – chalk régime. Now there is far more seeing and doing to appeal to visual and kinaesthetic people.

Auditory thinkers like to be right. Maybe we forget our visual skills and see only black and white; and because we only know how to deal in words, words are all we have to deal with – we may pay scant attention to different interpretations of those words or to what we observe in the speakers.

Until we stop to think about it, we may be unaware of our internal dialogue. There it is, telling us to be careful, that we are going to make fools of ourselves, that we are idiots and all the other things it says in order to keep us safe from harm (it may be our voice or someone else's – perhaps a parent, who also had a vested interest in protecting us).

The interesting thing about internal dialogue is that it is at its strongest when we are using foveal vision, in other words, when our vision is concentrated. When we allow our eyes to relax and go into peripheral vision, where we can see most of the 180 degrees in front of us, instead of being concentrated on a particular point, our internal dialogue leaves us in peace.

> If you concentrate on one word in the middle of the paragraph above, you will bring that word into sharper focus while the words on the outside edge will be more or less out of your awareness as individual words, and you may also be aware of internal dialogue about whether you are doing this right, what you can see and whether what I have said is true. Whereas if you relax your vision, you will lose the clarity of the word you chose to focus on, but the shapes of the rest of the words in the paragraph will come into your awareness.

Another way of comparing peripheral and foveal vision is to imagine that you are driving. Foveal vision would not be useful because, if you are concentrating exclusively on a point ahead of you, you would be unaware of any dangers from the side or of what was in your mirrors. We need peripheral vision to widen our awareness. Perhaps the cry 'Look out!' is an unconscious order to get out of foveal and into peripheral vision in order to increase the visual field and therefore our awareness of danger.

John McWhirter, an NLP trainer, produced a fascinating theory about what happens at meetings depending on who is there. Imagine a committee discussing a possible project. Since it has nothing to do with food, aromatherapy and so on,

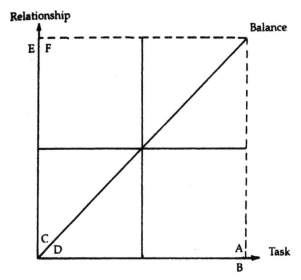

Who does what at meetings?

we shall use only the three main systems to describe who is at the meeting:

- A, visual, for it
- B, visual, against it
- C, auditory, for it
- D, auditory, against it
- E, kinaesthetic, for it
- F, kinaesthetic, against it

Predominantly visual people see the task and go for it. They are gaze hounds, hunting by sight, and so concentrated on the goal that they cannot hear you trying to call them off. A friend of mine could never let his whippets off the lead where there might be anything to hunt because, once they had seen their quarry, they were gone for hours or days and came back torn to shreds; there was nothing he or barbed wire could do to stop them.

Predominantly auditory people stick, as you would expect, to the words: they go by the book, according to the rules.

They are so concentrated on getting things right that they forget about the relationship with the people involved, and the importance of the task itself takes second place to the correctness of detail.

Kinaesthetic people need to feel comfortable, so they will concentrate on the relationship with other people at the expense of the task; as opposed to the visuals who will concentrate on the task rather than the relationship, and the auditories, who are sticking to the book and going nowhere.

In the first diagram on page 87 we see that A and B have gone for their respective tasks: A is for and B is against. They have ignored everything and everybody in their pursuit; they are as far as possible away from 'Relationship' and are now probably at daggers drawn. E and F have been busy with their relationship. They have agreed to disagree, and are as far as possible away from the task. They are now probably having a cup of tea together and disturbing the rest of the meeting with their chatter and laughter. C and D are bogged down with fine detail. The task is nowhere nearer to completion, and the thought of the relationship has probably not occurred to them as relevant. They are arguing about how, if the other

Balancing task and relationship at meetings

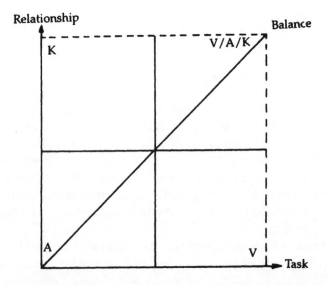

side gets its way, so-and-so or such-and-such a thing will be adversely affected.

The ideal outcome for any meeting is to achieve the task and maintain the relationship. For this, we need a balance of all three systems: people who can see the task, hear the words and and be aware of other people's feelings. People with this balance are easy to work with and get things done with the minimum of fuss.

I ran a workshop on negotiation just before discovering this theory. I showed it to the same people the next week, just producing it as an interesting theory that John had worked out. They thought about it for a bit and said, 'That is exactly how we behaved last week!' And they were right. The scenario was that each had won a free holiday and the only difficulty was that they all had to go together. Out of five of them, two wanted to go on a photographic safari to Kenya – and they ended up choosing a trip on the Orient Express. Imagine, two people with a passion for wide open spaces, allowing themselves to be talked into being cooped up in a train for days or weeks. One of the safari people was kinaesthetic, so he was not prepared to upset anyone. The other one finally gave up on the grounds of lack of seniority: he was years younger than the others and his internal dialogue was telling him that he 'should' agree with his elders. The one who wanted to go on the Orient Express was auditory, and stuck to her guns through thick and thin – there was never any question of her giving in.

Now that you are aware of your predominant system, and have discovered how useful the others can be as well, you can enjoy playing 'Spot the System' at work, at play and in the media. You can also enjoy the flexibility of having all your systems at your disposal, and joining other people in theirs to maintain the relationship and get the task done.

A balance of all our learning systems not only allows us to learn fast and effectively, it also helps us to get on with other people, because we can experience their models of the world. This is the equipment we were born with, so let's use it to make our lives as simple and as much fun as possible. We could start by allowing ourselves some more self-indulgence.

You could take some private time off, just for you, and settle yourself somewhere warm and comfortable, safe and secure, with a 'Do not Disturb' sign on the door and the telephone switched off; with some nice music in the background, where you can relax and daydream as though you had all the time in the world. You could even put these words on tape for yourself, using just the right warm, comfortable tone of voice that you would like to hear, and reading in the slow, relaxed way that will appeal to your unconscious mind, leaving just the right amount of pauses for your mind to process, all the way through your body, the words that you are saying. And perhaps your conscious mind is going to find all this very boring, so you might like to allow it to wander off, knowing that it can come back whenever you need it.

And when you are *really* comfortable, *really* relaxed, and feeling *really* safe, and perhaps beginning to become aware of your breathing, you can allow yourself to close your eyes and begin to become aware of the sounds around you, of the position of your body, as you gradually become more and more relaxed, and begin to experience how this relaxation is spreading through your body, from the top of your head, to the tip of your nose, to the tips of your fingers and the tips of your toes. And maybe your body would like to readjust itself to these feelings of comfort and relaxation.

And as you become more and more aware of your brain and body as a whole system, you might like to get in touch with the different parts of your body. You might like to start with your left big toe. And I wonder how your left big toe will react to this greeting. I wonder whether it will feel warmer, or cooler, or lighter or heavier; I don't know – it is your left big toe. I wonder which part of your left big toe you have chosen to get in touch with: maybe it is the whole toe, maybe it is the top end, maybe it is the middle bit or maybe you are in contact with just one cell. Whatever you have chosen, it is a system, which is part of a greater system, which is part of an even greater system: cell, joint, toe, foot, leg and so on; each system working for itself as part of a greater system, and all those systems working for you.

And I wonder what would happen if you gradually got in touch with every part of your body: all your toes, your feet, your lower legs, your thighs – taking as long as you like with each contact so that you can allow yourself to become more and more aware of every part of you, as you acknowledge each part and each part returns the greeting in whatever way it chooses. I wonder what you are becoming aware of as your thoughts move up through your hips and your stomach and into your backbone. I wonder if you are sinking deeper and deeper into relaxation or floating higher and higher as you gradually become free of all tension. I don't know how you and your body communicate with each other. I wonder if your stomach is rumbling as it lets go of tension. I wonder if you can feel slight twitches as your muscles readjust themselves to all these feelings. I wonder if your breathing has become slower and deeper as the relaxation spreads up the length of your spine, through your rib cage, into your lungs.

And I wonder if your shoulders and your neck are aware that in a moment or two they are going to be allowed to let go and join the rest of your body in this comfortable state, so that they can allow this new freedom to extend down through your arms and hands and into the tips of your fingers and thumbs.

And I am curious as to whether you will be aware, as your thoughts move up into your head, how the left and right sides of your body can readjust to each other. These two symmetrical systems that were created to work together may be allowing themselves to rebalance after a long time of separation. Perhaps you are experiencing a loosening, a freedom in that spot where your neck joins your head, that channel where all the information flows in both directions, from your brain to your body and from your body to your brain.

Maybe you are becoming aware of a lightness and a clarity both inside and outside your head as your eyes allow themselves to relax, and that relaxation spreads to your forehead and the whole of your scalp; as the strongest muscle in your body – your jaw muscle – relaxes, and allows the contours of your cheeks to soften; as you feel the saliva in your mouth and feel your tongue fill and spread itself in the gap between your upper and lower teeth.

And maybe, when you have allowed yourself as much time as you need to really appreciate every part of your body, you might like to allow yourself to take another trip to a favourite place. This may be the same place that you chose last time or it may be somewhere quite different. I don't know where you will choose to go; all I do know is that you will choose somewhere that is exactly right for you in your present state of relaxation and curiosity. And while you are in this favourite place you will be able to see what you see in surprising detail; I wonder what special sight will catch your eyes. You will find that you will be able to hear what you hear with interest and curiosity; I wonder what particular sounds will resonate with you. You will be able to feel what you feel from the top of your head, to the tip of your nose, to the tips of your fingers and the tips of your toes; I wonder just how interesting and surprising it is to be connected to all of you. Maybe those feelings will bring back long-forgotten memories, and create new memories for your store of treasures, as you add the tastes and smells that belong in this favourite place, which is becoming even more fascinating to you, as you become more and more aware of it through all your senses. And I am curious about which smells will come to you from the past, the present and the future, and what sort of tastes you are experiencing or about to experience on this visit to your favourite place.

And I ask myself what would happen if you allowed yourself to go deep into the very inside of *you*, until you could become aware of that spark, that flame, that light, that brightness that has always been there, but maybe has allowed itself to become a little dimmed over time. I don't know whether you will *do whatever you need to do* to allow that brilliance to show itself again, so that you may be deeply aware of its shining presence within you, and I don't know how long you will choose to stay with that brilliance in your favourite place, or what discoveries you will make while you are there; nor do I know what you will choose to do while you are there or how best you can *enjoy your self*. All I do know is that when you choose to come back to the here and now, you will feel alert, alive, relaxed and very *pleased with your self*, knowing that you can do this again and again whenever you want; and the more often that you do it, the better you will feel.

This sort of self-indulgence is the perfect way to set yourself up for a busy time, to unwind after a heavy day, to wake yourself up for a party, to drift off easily to sleep – and almost anything else you can think of. We can give ourselves permission to enjoy it on the grounds that the more time we spend in exploration, the easier we will be able to learn.

Pause for Thought:
How Will You Know?

In our first pause for thought I asked you what you wanted; the question here is 'How will you know when you have got it?' What will you see and hear and feel and taste and smell? What will your evidence be for your success at certain steps along the way? If you were playing around with your visual skills, what would your evidence be that they were increasing? Would you find yourself noticing things that you had never noticed before? Would you find that you could remember pictures more easily? Would you find that you were more struck by colour than you used to be? Would you become aware that your peripheral vision was improving?

If you want something like a new job or promotion, the evidence is simple: you will know that you have got it because someone will tell you. If, on the other hand, your outcome is to have more self-confidence, how will you know when you have got it? Will other people pay more attention to you? Will other people look smaller in your mind's eye? Will your internal pictures be bigger or smaller, brighter or clearer than they are now? Will you be aware that you are speaking more slowly and calmly? Will you hear an internal voice telling you that you are doing well? Will you feel taller, lighter or warmer than you do now? Will there be a nice taste in your mouth or a nice smell in your nostrils? All these are just my suggestions, your evidence that you are achieving your outcome could be anything. However curious or silly your evidence may seem (you may see yourself swinging from

a chandelier, feeling champagne bubbles in your nostrils), it is
your evidence – that is what matters; that is how you will
know.

It is important to have some form of evidence procedure,
otherwise how will you know? Lazy learning is so easy that
you may be unaware at a conscious level of how much you are
learning. A woman once asked me to do something about the
feelings of persecution that she was experiencing when she
heard brakes squealing; she was convinced that those awful
noises were directed at her personally. I told her that I could
muffle all the offending brakes in her area, but it would cost
her £10,015.47; alternatively, if she felt that she could not
afford that, she could do the job herself by simply filtering out
the sounds. Doubtless thinking me uncaring and unhelpful,
she went away. When I enquired the next day how the squealing brakes were, she asked me crossly what I was talking
about: her brain had done the job so effectively that she had
forgotten she had ever had the problem. This is all very fine,
but most of us like to be able to look back with pride along
the path we have taken and give ourselves the occasional pat
on the back when we see how far we have come. We all need a
sense of achievement to carry us forward into the next dream;
a treasure chest full of things that we have done and done
well; treasures that we can draw upon in the future. You
might like to pause for a moment to take account of everything that you have learned since you started to read this
book: everything you have learned about yourself, everything
that you have learned about other people and everything that
you have discovered since taking these learnings out into the
world and making use of them. You can become aware that
you have learned all these things without trying at all.

And the next question is. How do you know that you
know? For example, how do you know that you want to do
something? The information has to come from somewhere.
Do you see a bright, attractive picture in your mind's eye? Do
you have a voice telling you that you want to do it in your
mind's ear? Do you feel yourself being drawn towards whatever it is? Do you get a particular taste in your mouth or smell

in your nostrils when you think about it? Or is all your evidence completely different?

How do you know that someone loves, likes or appreciates you? I was working with a couple who loved each other dearly, but their marriage was in serious trouble. I asked her how she knew that he loved her; 'Because of the melting look he gives me' came the reply without hesitation.

His reply to the same question was 'Because of the tone of her voice'. Mr and Mrs Doasyouwouldbedoneby had the most positive of intentions: she had been giving him the melting look that *she* knew was proof of love, but he could not hear any evidence; he had been telling her that he loved her, in the tone of voice that *he* knew was irrefutable evidence, but she saw nothing to prove it.

We all have different evidence procedures and it is useful to find out what our family, friends and colleagues need so that we can provide it for them, and to tell them ours, so that they can provide it for us.

Some Tricks of the Trade

THE BIG F

The story goes that it took Thomas Edison 1,000 attempts before he succeeded in creating a light bulb that worked, and that when somebody asked him if he had become depressed by his 999 failures, he replied indignantly, 'I did not have 999 failures; I discovered 999 ways how not to make a light bulb.' In examination terms we all know what the big F stands for, and, in NLP we believe that there is no failure, there is only feedback – in other words, there is always something to be learned from the experience. We also operate on the principle that if whatever we are doing is not working, it is time to try something different.

It takes a lot of effort not to learn: to close down all five input channels, and keep them closed, to search frantically for non-stop displacement activities, to listen intently to our internal voices telling us that we are stupid, to argue internally with everything that we see, hear or feel, to dig ourselves deeper and deeper into a slough of despond or whatever means we choose to employ; it is hard work, and yet we persevere, we *succeed* in not learning.

The question that I would ask now is: are you happy to go on giving yourself a hard time, or would you like to relax, sit back and allow yourself to learn. If you would like to give up the unequal struggle of not learning, let us think about how feedback opens up new options for us to play with. Once we have discovered that what we are doing does not work, we are no longer bound by any preconceptions; we can try anything we like. What would happen, for example, if you invented a new, fun way of committing something to memory: if you drew pictures instead of writing notes, wrote silly poems to remind you of things, sang the information to a favourite tune, and did any of these things while you were standing on your head? The more creative you are, the more of your neurology you invest, the easier learning will become. What is the French for 'sticky tape'? If my story appealed to you, you will remember; if it did not, you won't – it is as simple as that.

Your part in the system

Because our internal state decides whether we do or do not learn, and because it is generally some other part of the system that can create a bad state in us if we allow it to, the first magic trick that I want to demonstrate is how we can have choices in our reactions to other people instead of automatically feeling bad. It is called a 'Meta Mirror', and was developed by Robert Dilts and Todd Epstein. You can use it for anybody that you do not like; anybody that you are having trouble with, anyone who has a bad effect on you or with whom you do not feel comfortable. You will need some space in which to move around. It may also help to enrol a friend to read out the instructions. Give yourself plenty of time in each position to be aware of what is going on. And be kind to yourself.

1 Choose a spot where you feel comfortable, where you can stand, and imagine the other person standing opposite you. We'll call this first position. Stand on that spot, look at the other person in your imagination and experience what is going on inside you, with the other person standing opposite you; maybe you are talking; maybe you are glaring at each other – I don't know.

When you are aware of what is going on inside you, step out of that spot, shaking off those feelings and leaving them behind.

2 Step into the other person's shoes and *become* him or her for a moment. (You already know how to do this: just take on the other person's physiology and *be* them). Look back at where you were standing and see yourself there, as you were. How does it feel to *be* that other person looking at you? Experience what is going on inside you as you take the part of that other person, and describe it as the other person: 'I see ... I hear ... I feel ...'

When you are aware of what it is like to be the other person in this exchange, step out of that spot, which we will call second position, shaking off the feelings and leaving them behind.

3 Choose a third position, where you can observe you and the other person from the outside. You will become aware of how they form a system: how each one's behaviour affects the other. Lean back slightly and fold your arms: you are the choreographer watching the dance between those two people. Describe what is happening, referring to the You over there by name and saying what you are doing, and what the other person is doing, and why you think each is behaving like that.

4 Now you can leave the choreographer behind and move to a fourth position, where you can become aware of the relationship between the You as choreographer and the You on the firing line. Are those two Yous the same age, or is one older than the other? Are they the same size, or is one smaller than the other? Is one wiser than the other? Is one more vulnerable than the other? What differences do you notice between the two of them? You can spend as much time as you like in this position.

When you have discovered the differences, ask yourself what those two Yous think of each other. Maybe they get on well together or maybe they irritate each other. I don't know. All I do know is that each has resources that the other needs. Perhaps the older one has wisdom and detachment; perhaps the younger one has openness and curiosity – I don't know what you will discover. Describe the differences you observe in this fourth position; for example, 'the Fred/Freda in third position does not get drawn into it emotionally, whereas the Fred/Freda in first position feels that he/she is being attacked.' What you will discover now is that the You who has been having the difficulty with the other person is probably not the right person to respond in any useful way to what is going on in that interaction.

Then you can ask yourself what would happen if the You in third position changed places with the You in first position; in other words, if the wiser, more detached You took over this difficult situation. If that seems a good plan, you can go back and pick up the You in third position and take that You into first position. I don't know where you would like to put the You who was originally in first position; a colleague of mine found that she was so small in first position, that she put that 'her' into her pocket to keep her safe. It is up to you to decide where that You will be safest and most comfortable, and yet always available with all those wonderful resources whenever you need them.

You may decide that you need to go out to a fifth position to get an even wider perspective, and that the You in fourth position is the one who would best cope with the situation. That fifth position can be wherever you choose – maybe on the floor, or on the ceiling – so that you can see the interaction from a different angle. You will choose the best place for yourself.

When you have selected the most appropriate You to be in first position, you can stand there once again, facing the other person. Take a deep breath and notice how everything has changed. When you are fully aware of how different you feel, shake that off and step into the other person's shoes again. Look back at yourself and be aware of the changes that you observe. Try to treat this new you in whatever way that other person does, and notice the changes in your reactions. You will discover that the situation has completely changed for the other person too.

When you have fully appreciated the changes, step out of the other person's shoes, shake him or her off, step back into first position and enjoy your self.

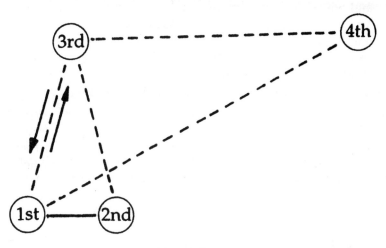

Meta Mirror

The reason that this works so well is because we are physically separating the problem space into its various compartments, so that no one position can contaminate another. It gives us a chance to be in our bodies and really experience what is going on in each position instead of trying to sort out the situation in our heads and getting into a muddle, because it is so complicated when our feelings slither from one situation, where they do belong, to another where they don't. Describing what is going on in each position also helps to keep the sorting clean.

You can use this piece of magic anywhere at any time. Ian McDermott recounts how someone was giving him a hard time at a dinner party, so he left the room for a moment, did a quick Meta Mirror, came back and enjoyed the rest of the evening.

THINKING ABOUT CRITICISM

Verbal criticism starts early in life when we are called 'naughty' or 'bad'; and it is not long before we get it in black and white. Neil was bright as a button: you only had to tell him or show him something once and he understood it. He had, however, been expelled from several schools, and a note from one of them read: 'We try to find some good in every child, but, unfortunately, with Neil, we failed.' Neil's only problem was that school wasn't challenging him, so he got bored; if we leave a young dog alone in the house all day, we can hardly blame it if it chews our shoes.

To interpret criticism usefully, we need to think again about the different logical levels of thought – identity, belief, capability, behaviour, environment – and ask ourselves what each criticism actually means.

'A is lazy.' Let us ask the creator of this identity-level statement what it means, precisely.

'Well, he never does any work.'

'Never?'

'Well, not never, but most of the time.'

'How much of the time?'

'Every afternoon.'

Without going into further detail about how we know that A does not do any work in the afternoons, we have already established that this statement is about a behaviour and has nothing to do with who A is. If we continue with our careful questioning, we may discover that A is grossly underemployed and has finished all his work by lunchtime, or that making paper planes is the way he distracts his conscious mind when he needs to think. Whatever we may discover, it does not relate to his identity. 'B is aggressive.' We ask some questions, and may discover that making a lot of noise is the only strategy that B has for getting people to listen to him. Behaviour again.

Naughty, bad and rude are all adjectives following the verb 'to be'. They are all identity statements made about the young, and the young, being sensitive, believe that these pronouncements are the truth about *who* they are, whereas a little judicious questioning reveals that they are really about behaviour. If criticism is made at an identity level, we take it at an identity level, unless we know how to stop and think about it. Statements like 'You are irresponsible/a poor communicator/too possessive' make people feel bad about themselves – about who they are – and this may result in even more erratic behaviour or in their dismissing the message we are trying to get across. If, as your passenger, I am terrified by the speed at which we are travelling, I need to do something to alleviate the situation. I can either tell you that you are a bad driver and risk the consequence that you might drive even faster just to show me how good you are, or I can tell the truth and say, 'This speed terrifies me. Can we slow down a bit?' Which statement would get the message across to you and have the desired effect?

Whatever the situation, it needs to be dealt with. You matter to me, and I do not want to make you feel bad. However, I matter even more to me, so I am not going to suffer in silence. My outcome is simply to get my message across to you, and for you to alter your behaviour so that I will feel better. We need to remember that identity-level criticism of us comes from a basic need that the other person has not yet learned how to express: something that we have done makes them feel bad, and it is easier for them to shift those bad feelings onto us than it is to address them.

As a learning experience, I took Caroline and Sylvain to visit Jemima Parry-Jones, an outstanding falconer. The children knew nothing about falconry or any of the vocabulary related to it, and I just chucked them in the deep end and left them to it: I was there to answer questions, but not to teach. They spent the day watching a varied assortment of different birds being flown: owls, sea eagles, vultures, peregrines and luggers, and the next day they put their findings together systemically:

- where and when each bird hunted,
- what each bird hunted,
- how each hunted,
- why each hunted in that particular way,
- who each bird was,

and they realized that Jemima's training was so effective because it was done at an identity level: each bird mattered to her as an individual, and she treated each one with the respect due to an individual.

When Caroline's mother came to take them home she made an identity-level remark that might formerly have cut her daughter to the quick. Caroline just grinned at me and said, 'and I wonder what logical level I'm supposed take that at.' Caroline was twelve; she knew how to think, and had choices about how to react. If we have no choices, we will run our automatic 'coping with criticism' program, which is geared to stop us from feeling bad. Whatever this program is, it may involve some sort of systems close-down, and we will not learn anything from the situation.

ASKING QUESTIONS

Why do I need to learn this?

I could never see the point of learning dates at school, so I never bothered, and it was not until years later that I realized that dates do have their uses in the greater scheme of things if we want to know what was going on in different places at the same time. For example, it may be interesting to realize that all Jane Austen's village and family dramas take place during the Napoleonic Wars. Ask yourself 'Why do I need to learn this?', and if you cannot think of an answer, ask whoever is telling you to learn it. If you do not get a valid answer, you can decide whether or not you are going to bother.

What do I need to learn?

Given a weighty textbook, a mass of revision, a new subject – whatever – we need an outcome, otherwise we are back in the desert in evening dress on a camel. Knowing *what* we need to learn not only gives us a direction, it also saves hours of wasted time.

I don't understand

I once asked a young client who went to a private school what would happen if he told the teacher that he did not understand. He looked at me in horror and told me that he would get 'blasted out'. I asked who the teacher worked for; the answer was 'the school'. I then enquired who paid the school fees. When the boy realized that his parents paid the school to pay the teachers to educate him, he was happy to stand up for his rights.

How do I do that?

We are given all sorts of instructions like 'Listen!', 'Pay Attention!', 'Concentrate!', and everybody assumes that we know how to do these things. For example, how would you teach people to listen, especially if they have never listened in their lives? What would they have to do to be able to listen? If you are told to do something that you do not know how to do, ask. You may have to do this diplomatically or whoever you are asking might think you were making fun of them.

Which questions to ask?

Thinking of the logical levels, the questions we will need to ask are: where, when, what, how, why, who and who else? You will find that you are now so aware of all the different levels that the questions will raise themselves automatically as you come to recognize more and more sloppy thinking. Listen to politicians expounding, and become aware of the levels at which they are or are not answering questions.

What would it be like to be riding on a light beam? This question supposedly came to Einstein in a mathematics class when he was bored. I imagine that he would have got a fairly unenthusiastic response if he had voiced such a ridiculous idea to his teacher, but it was this question that led him into physics and subsequently to his theory of relativity, which has transformed our concepts of time and space.

Ask 'crazy' questions; you have no idea where they may lead you. If anyone tells you to shut up or stop being stupid, you can go and find someone else who is more interested in thinking.

I wonder why so many of our expressions about intelligence refer to light:

- bright
- brilliant
- it dawned on me
- I saw the light
- a glimpse of the blinding obvious
- becoming enlightened
- being delighted
- clarity
- lucidity
- breadth of vision

And why did Aladdin's genie come out of a lamp?

What would happen if you did ... ?

This question, as Ian McDermott would say, is more than worth the price of this book.

- You have waited three weeks for the repair man to come to fix your heating, or the telephone engineer to install a new line, and when he arrives he cannot do some final essential part of the job because of 'company policy'.

- You cannot tell someone that you do not understand something.
- You cannot tell an overpowering bully to get lost.

'What would happen if you did?' is a question that gets people thinking about their limiting beliefs, and realizing that maybe they can, after all. When you ask someone this question, do it gently if you want to stay friends.

OUR EFFECT UPON OTHER PEOPLE

We learn how to establish rapport with other people by mirroring and matching their behaviour so that they will feel comfortable with us. Mirroring and matching are behaviour level activities, and I believe that a basic human need is to be acknowledged as a person. So I can go through the whole rigmarole of mirroring and matching you, but if you as a person do not matter to me, none of my skills or techniques is going to work. Rapport is an identity-level business, as Caroline and Sylvain discovered at the falconry. Todd Epstein added a valuable rider to this glimpse of the blinding obvious: 'and, if I don't matter to you, it could be because I don't matter to myself', which gives us permission not to have to get on with everybody. So if Joe Soap is so wrapped up in his own sense of worthlessness, we do not have to join him in his model of the world and create the same sense of worthlessness in ourselves. And we can allow ourselves to feel OK about not wanting to get involved with him.

Don Juan, the Yacqui Indian medicine man with whom the anthropologist Carlos Castaneda spent many years as an apprentice, caught and held Castaneda's attention by looking at him straight in the right eye. Try it, and see what happens.

As we cannot go around asking complete strangers what their evidence procedure is for knowing that we like them, we need to acknowledge people visually, auditorially and kinaesthetically if we are to be sure of making the connection.

In other words, we need to look at them, to match the tone of their voice, and to match their movements and/or breathing and perhaps nod our heads slightly in time with their gestures or the words they are stressing. (If you watch friends deep in conversation, you will see that this is exactly what they are doing unconsciously.) You could start by trying these techniques with complete strangers, and discover how interesting they are. Then you could try them with people you thought you had nothing in common with and see what develops, or you could just try them with everybody.

These techniques work because we are making contact at a subconscious level. The other person is not consciously aware of what we are doing; all they will be aware of is that a bond has been established, and their behaviour will change to reinforce that bond. Even the smallest of nods will register in other people's peripheral vision. My clients enjoy trying this at meetings, because the meetings suddenly become so much more alive and interesting.

PROBLEM SOLVING

We cannot solve a problem at the same level at which it was created. I was woken at 3.30 one morning in my hotel in Santa Cruz by the steady sound of dripping. Water was cascading into my bedroom and bathroom: something was overflowing upstairs. I scattered receptacles and bath towels and then dialled the room upstairs – no answer, so I rang the front desk. The people there were charming and very sympathetic, offering to deliver receptacles and bath towels, and move me to another room; but because the maintenance man would not be on duty until 8.30, they could not do anything about the overflow. They were prepared to do anything in their power, on the same level, but they would not go up to a higher floor to deal with the cause.

If X upsets people by shouting at them, gagging him may make life easier for everyone else, but he will be worse when we take the

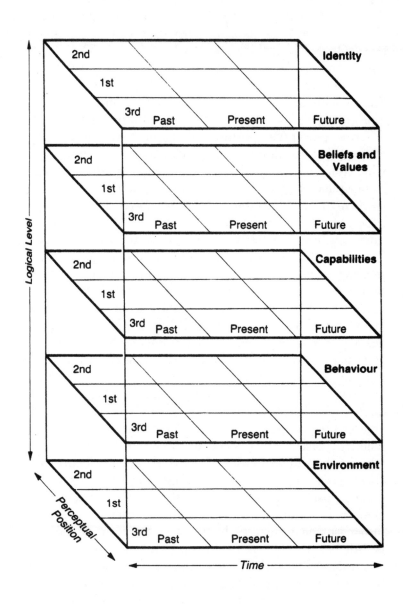

The "Jungle Gym"

gag off. We need to work our way up the logical levels to discover the cause of his behaviour. Is he unable to keep calm under stress? Does he believe that it is the only way to get anyone to listen to him? Is it an identity question: 'They do not think I am important?' Or is it something completely different? Whatever the answer may be, we will not find it at the 'what' level.

The illustration on page 109 shows Robert Dilts and Todd Epstein's Jungle Gym. As you can see, it has the five different logical levels, each with past, present and future, and the three different perceptual positions that you used for the Meta Mirror. First position is you, associated into your body, being who you are, seeing what you see, hearing what you hear, feeling what you feel in the problem situation; second position is when you step into someone else's shoes and become them, experiencing everything through their eyes, ears and feelings; third position is when you are outside the situation, being detached and objective about it. Outside the Jungle Gym, considering the problem as a whole, you could think of yourself in fourth position. It is an excellent toy for problem solving. If you want to have one made, mine measures 12 x 12 x 18 inches (30 x 30 x 45 centimetres) and each of the forty-five squares has a hole in it which will hold a ping-pong ball.

Remember the chemist who was so angry with me? The immediate problem was first position, present, behaviour: 'I am bewildered now; this person is giving me a hard time and I do not understand why' – place a ball in that hole. If I want to enlarge the problem space and put a ball in second position, identity, present, I can step into his shoes and think about who he is in this situation. I discover that his identity as a chemist is threatened by my equating cookery to chemistry; in second position, beliefs, present, the thought comes up that cookery is a mundane capability that women have. If we go into past and future, perhaps the last person who tried to belittle his talents took over his job. If I then move into first position, beliefs, future, I can check out whether this theory I have just invented will be useful for me in the future; if yes, I can try on my first position, future, behaviour for size. Then I can move out to third position and check where and when this choice of new behaviour will be appropriate, how it will appear to outsiders, and so on. The more we enlarge the problem space, the clearer the solution becomes. Once you have defined the problem space with the ping-pong balls, you can start to look for the solution from any space. You may prefer to go to third position straightaway and view the problem with detachment. You may find the answers at the where-when level – X gives you a hard time when he's had a row with his wife or when you breathe garlic at him after lunch. You may find them at the what level: from the outside, you can see that you and Y are behaving in exactly the same way – each is being equally defensive, so the situation is getting more and more tense. Play around in the Jungle Gym and you will be surprised what you discover.

TREASURE HUNTING

Think about something that you really enjoy doing. It may be a hobby, it may be something to do with work – it can be anything you like from beekeeping to yodelling. When you have decided what to think about, you can allow yourself to become aware of just how much you have learned about that subject while you were simply enjoying yourself: how much you have learned from experience, and how much you have discovered out of sheer curiosity by asking questions, experimenting, researching, and so on.

Publishers ask people to write books about their hobbies. 'Who, me?' these hobbyists ask in astonishment, having never considered themselves in any way qualified to expound on something that for them is simply fun; they are amazed to discover that they are considered to be authorities on the subject.

When you have carefully considered the wealth and depth of your knowledge, you can think of something ordinary that you have learned about by yourself: running a house, getting on with other people, understanding cats – things that you learned how to do without being taught. How many things can you think of that fall into this category? You might like to make a list, and also a list of learnings through your hobbies.

Then there are all those things that we talked about earlier, like learning to crawl, to feed yourself, to walk, to talk: everything that you learned from the moment you were born until you went to school. You can make another list, which will take you a long time if you do it thoroughly.

When you are fully aware of how much you have learned for yourself, make a line on the ground, a timeline, on which you decide which direction is your future, and which is your past. Which way do you want to face as you look forward to your future?

You may find it useful to get someone to read the instructions to you as you do the exercise.

| Past | Present | Future |

When you are ready, you can step on to the line in the spot that you have chosen to represent the present, and just be in the here and now, looking forward to your future, to what you have decided that you want. When your future is clear in front of you, you can start your treasure hunt by walking slowly backwards along your timeline into your past, back to all those moments when you learned with ease and enjoyment because you simply wanted to know. Just walk back along the line and your body will know where to stop for each particular learning moment.

As you get to each moment, pause, take a deep breath and experience what is going on inside you at that moment. What are you seeing? What are you hearing? What are you feeling, tasting and smelling while you are learning so easily? See what you see, hear what you hear and feel what you feel in that learning moment, so that you really experience what it is like to be in learning mode. You might like to do something that will fix all this in your neurology: as that awareness starts to heighten in each spot (maybe as you are taking your deep breath), you could press your thumb and forefinger together, or squeeze your ear or wiggle your nose. This will act as your own magic button, so you can bring this learning state back to you whenever you need it; it might be wise to choose something that you can do in public without everyone thinking that you have finally flipped.

As you go back along the line picking up all the treasures by way of learning experiences (and pressing your magic button as you start to become aware of each treasure, as everything that goes with that internal state comes into action), you may find some dark spots on the line. You can deal with these in any way that you like: you can shine some light on them, step over them, walk around them – you will know what is best.

Continue along the line, stopping at all the learning moments and picking up everything that you experience there, until you get to your very earliest learning moment where you can stop and look along the line you have walked and at all the treasures you have discovered, which you can carry forward to the present and into your future.

When you are truly aware of them all, you can start moving towards the present once more, stopping again at each learning spot and pressing your magic button. While you are doing this, I wonder how many more learning spots you will become aware of as you move up the line again towards the present, and how much lighter any dark spots will look with the extra brightness you are bringing to them with the knowledge and awareness you have acquired. You can take as long as you like in each spot, as long as you need to enjoy it fully.

When you get back to the present, with your store of treasures from the past, you can look forward to the future that you have decided that you want for yourself – at your dream, and the dream beyond your dream – knowing that you are capable of learning anything that you want to learn, because you have brought the proof from your past back to the present with you. If you like, you can press your magic button and walk forward until you reach that goal on your future timeline, and experience what it feels like to have already achieved it; and you can look back to the present and see how you got there, becoming aware of the stepping stones that you took along the way. When you have fully experienced what it feels like to have achieved that goal, you can walk back to the present, savouring all those good feelings. When you get to the present, turn and look at your goals again and see how much simpler and more fun everything looks. You might like to attach yourself to your goals with a golden thread or a beam of light, or anything that is going to draw you inexorably towards them – knowing that at any stage you can change, add to and improve upon them.

Your magic button is now available to you whenever you want to be in a true learning state; whenever you want your natural ability to bring every part of you into learning mode, just press the button and it will happen automatically.

And now is the time to have a complete break to allow your unconscious mind to process its discoveries.

SOFTWARE FOR READING AND WRITING

An important piece of software is how we think about time; in other words, where do you see the past and where do you see the future in your mind's eye? Some people know exactly where they see them; others have to think about it for a bit before they become aware that they see the past in one direction and the future in another. If you are still wondering where you see or feel past and future, try the following experiment.

Think about something you did last week, something you did last month and something you did last year. Then think about something you are planning to do next week, next month and next year. Choose something routine, like cleaning your teeth.

How do you know which things you have already done and which are still in your imagination? Your brain has arranged an excellent filing system, so that you know at once which is which, because the pictures, feelings and sounds will be in different places.

Another way of discovering how your brain organizes time for you is to imagine that one thing you must do today is to telephone me and wish me a happy birthday. You know that you will get my answering machine, so you will have no memories of what I have said to you. *How will you know when you have done it?*

Most right-handed people keep the past somewhere on their left and the future somewhere on their right. When you ask them questions that involve memory, their eyes will move to the left – either to look at pictures or to hear sounds. When

How our eyes process a line of text

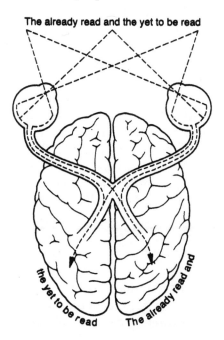

The already read and the yet to be read

the yet to be read

The already read and

you ask them to construct a picture of something they have never seen or a sound they have never heard, their eyes will move to the right. For example, what do you think my voice sounds like? Where did your eyes go as you thought about that question? In languages that are written from left to right, like English, what we have read is in the past, on the left; and what we are about to read is in the future, on the right.

Reading is a complicated process and our eyes are extraordinarily clever about making it simpler. As you will see from the diagram on page 115 the peripheral vision of each eye checks what you have just read to see whether what you are reading now makes sense in relation to what you have just read; and, at the same time, the peripheral vision of each eye checks what you are about to read to ensure that what you are reading now will still make sense.

When working with a client who had been branded 'dyslexic' and was at a special school, I noticed that as I asked him questions about the past, his eyes went up to the right. Interested, I checked where he kept his timeline by asking him some of the questions I have just asked you. I then explained to him how our eyes work when we read and how, when we are reading, the past is on the left and the future is on the right. He was very interested, so I asked him what would happen if he changed his timeline round, and put his past on the left and his future on the right. There was a short pause, then: 'Wow! I can read! It's so easy!' Since then, I have found that all my clients with reading or writing difficulties kept their past on the right and the future on the left. This method of filing does not necessarily mean that one will have problems with reading; I know lots of people with right – left timelines who never had any such difficulties.

I was once asked to help someone who could not make any plans: she kept the past in front of her and the future behind her, so she had nothing to look forward to. There are endless variations in timelines. I have a colleague who can tell you exactly when everything happened: in her imagination she keeps her memories on different coloured scrolls in different coloured jars, according to date – brilliant! But dates are not that important to me and I could not be bothered with all that clutter; I like my memories in instantly available pictures.

I decided that I needed two timelines: one to live in and one for planning. I keep my planning line out in front of me, so that I do not have to keep turning round to check on learnings from the past. You can choose what is best for you – it is your brain.

Spelling

Ask good spellers to spell a word for you, and they will either look up or straight ahead to see a picture of the word, consciously or unconsciously. More creative spellers will look from side to side, in order to pick up the sounds of the word. Spelling phonetically is not very effective in English: 'P' stands for pheasant, ptarmigan and psychology; it sounds as if I come from grape written; and what about the person who won the pullet surprise? (If these last two have confused you completely, say them to somebody else: your listeners will understand at once because, unlike you, they will not have been confused by seeing the words.) Good spellers also check whether the word feels right by looking down (generally towards the hand they write with). Sometimes people are accused of reading just for the sake of looking for spelling mistakes. Not so – mis-spelt words seem to leap out of the page and hit them.

The trick to good spelling is to see the word. To learn a new word, we can hold it up so that we can see it clearly in the place where we keep our visual memory.

- Is it a long word, like 'cosmopolitan'?
- Is it a short word, like 'we'?
- Has it got the same sized letters, like 'enormous'?
- Has it got high letters, like 'filter'?
- Has it got low letters, like 'gypsy'?
- Has it got a mixture of these letters, like 'psychology'?
- Has it got double letters, like 'woolly?'

We can fix the word in our photographic memory by spelling it forwards, and then backwards. To make our mental picture easier to see, we can:

- make it bigger,
- make it brighter,
- bring it closer,
- change the colours of the letters and/or the background,
- put a frame round it (what sort of frame would you like?),
- put the picture in a special place, such as on a favourite animal, on a favourite poster, or on a favourite food.

You will discover whatever you need to do – experiment and have fun! Get the feel of the word by running your fingers along the letters, or writing it in the air or on your arm or leg – wherever you like. One of my colleagues, Christine Amato, who works for the Californian Education Authority, has teams of children going round the schools teaching other children how to spell.

Dictation

Edouard and Charles-Henri wanted to be better at dictation because their low marks were seriously undermining their overall averages and preventing them from being top of their classes: their pride was at stake. I asked Edouard who was best at dictation in his class: 'Céline', he said; so I told him to sit down and 'become' Céline. He took on the classic physiology of the good dictation taker: feet parallel and apart; sitting up straight and nicely balanced; with the paper at an angle of 45 degrees to the edge of the table. This was exactly what I expected, so I was surprised when Charles-Henri became Philippe (the best at dictation in his class): he was hunched over his paper, eyes down, with his left arm hiding what he was writing and, only when he was ready to go on, would he look up at me and grunt.

I dictated to them for five minutes, and then they got bored and reverted to being their usual selves. Then, just for interest, I gave them another five minutes' dictation. After this, they were in no mood for listening again and making corrections, so I gathered up their work to see what had happened. I could hardly believe my eyes: the first half, when they were modelling someone else, was tidy, well laid out and legible, with hardly a single mistake, whereas, the second half, when they were being themselves was a complete mess, almost illegible, and what I could read was wrong.

Charles-Henri's physiology was interesting. I have always thought that physiology was everything, but there he was, hunched over his work like a little old man and the results were brilliant. Maybe, after all, it was just a matter of distracting the conscious mind by modelling someone else. I wonder how different your experiences of learning would be if you tried this simple trick for every subject.

> All you have to do is to think about someone who is really good at whatever it is that you want to do, become that person for a while and discover what happens. Of course, you are you, and you do not want to change your identity, so, having discovered that it works, you can then ask yourself: What is the difference that makes the difference? In other words, what changes do you need to make in your physiology? What pictures do you need to make in your mind's eye? What sounds do you need to hear in your mind's ear? What were the differences that you noticed in what was going on inside you, when you were able to do whatever it was that you thought you could not do before?

Difficulties in reading and writing appear to be the main reason for labelling people as stupid and writing them off as a dead loss educationally. Fortunately, there are some people who are not prepared to bow to this 'superior' judgement and, as soon as they are free of the shackles of school, they strike out on their own and become great successes. Those with a less independent streak may well stay in the condemned cell for the rest of their lives: 'I am dyslexic, that is me – there is nothing to be done.'

BEWARE OF ADDERS!

Vying for first place in the list of things that we think we cannot learn is the big M – mathematics. We need to remember that maths was created to make life simpler rather than more difficult. Dr Caleb Gattegno created the concept of Algebricks or Cuisenaire Rods (the name varies according to manufacturer) to demonstrate that mathematics is just a code. The rods are different colours and different lengths according to the numbers that they represent. For example, the 1s are white cubes, the 2s are red and as long as two 1s laid side by side, and so on up to 10. By playing with them we can both see and feel how the concept of numbers works. We can discover how patterns emerge in our calculations, so we can save ourselves time and trouble by using the pattern, instead of doing the sum.

Introducing the abstract concept of arithmetic to the young brain can create terrible confusion. If you ask a child '5 + 6 = ?', the child can be forgiven for wondering '5 whats and 6 whats?' Algebra is much easier to understand because it is just a code to make life simpler. 'If there are 5 h(orses) and 6 c(ows) in a field, how many a(nimals) are there altogether?' can be written 5h + 6c = 11a to save time, space and effort.

Einstein's creative thinking process did not seem to involve mathematics at all: 'No really productive person thinks in such a paper fashion'. Robert Dilts maintains that if Einstein had not been able to represent the fruits of his imagination mathematically, his discoveries might have gone completely unnoticed by the scientific community. Genius is available to all of us, in whatever field we want to be creative. We just need to be able to enjoy coding our creativity in order to impress others, if that is what we want to do.

I remember laying Cuisenaire Rods out on the floor to illustrate an imaginary visit from the taxman to one of my clients who had a horror of algebra, and asking him to justify the supposed lack of profits for tax purposes. It was incredibly complicated, with carnivores costing so much to feed, and herbivores costing more in winter than in summer, and so on. After the client had successfully worked out his expenses and offset them against his income, I wrote the problem out alge-braically. He took one look at it and said, 'I can't do that!', but he had the grace to be embarrassed when he realized that he had, in fact, just done it. And, as he was a great one for an easy life, the discovery that algebra was purely a labour-saving device was a delight to him.

When we used Roman numerals, there was no symbol for zero, and therefore no idea of minus as being less than nothing; instead of having the following sequence of numbers, which the use of zero as an entity requires for balance:

$$-5, -4, -3, -2, -1, 0, 1, 2, 3, 4, 5$$

we had, instead, a sequence that presented a tangible, visible concept:

$$\tfrac{1}{5}, \tfrac{1}{4}, \tfrac{1}{3}, \tfrac{1}{2}, 1, 2, 3, 4, 5$$

an idea that we could do something with, instead of trying to get our brains round the thought of nothing and less than nothing.

A lot of people have difficulty with the concept of minus. To me it was always nonsensical, and the only thing I could relate it to was what would happen if I wrote a cheque for more money than I had in the bank. As for the concept that two minuses make a plus ... ! However nonsensical the concept of minus might appear, the trick is to remember that this is not reality, it is just a way of thinking. Every game has its rules and if we want to play the game, we can learn them.

The zero came from India, and was brought to Europe through Spain by the Arabs. Although the Church would have nothing to do with the idea, it caught on because trades-men found that it made their calculations much easier. Its adoption had a great effect upon thought: about ourselves as individuals, about death as a non-being, about the separation of heaven and earth, and maybe created the split between science and the arts, where one side is in opposition to the other instead of each being considered as a part of a contin-uum. In *Sacred Geometry*, Robert Lawlor describes the placing of zero before the number one as a number concept that is philosophically misleading. So, if you have had trouble with the concept of minus, you are in good company.

I remember a visual colleague telling me how mathematics was a closed book to him until he discovered geometry, and suddenly he could see what he was doing. Lawlor describes ancient geometry as a metaphor for universal order. Geometry is the study of what we know about already at a deep subconscious level. For example, some proportions please us and some do not, and we probably will not know why we have made these decisions. Given the choice of various rectangles, most people will light upon the one that contains the 'golden section' although they may never have heard of the concept. For sheer enjoyment and beauty, read *Sacred Geometry* and discover what geometry is really all about.

FOREIGN LANGUAGES

How did we manage to learn our native language? Here are some suggestions:

- We were born with a need to communicate in order to survive.
- Our attention was on the communication, not upon the language itself.
- We modelled other members of our family.
- We used trial and error until we were understood.
- All verbal communication was greeted with pride, joy and encouragement.
- We were learning in a safe environment.
- We were not constantly corrected.
- We have an inborn understanding of how language works.
- We did not have to learn regular verbs before being allowed to talk.
- We were allowed to learn in our own way.

Language is the conscious and unconscious expression of a culture that has evolved over time. A culture is a system within a system, and expressions vary from region to region because thought varies from region to region. In English, we look forward to things; in French, we wait for them with impatience; in German, we please ourselves at them; in Spanish, we delight ourselves in advance. These expressions illustrate profound differences in thought about the way we relate to the future. Language is about who we are, why we say the things that we say, and how we say them: where in our bodies the sounds come from.

Lazy language learning is a fascinating world. You have already learned so much about logical levels and modelling that you will be able to work wonders with the few tips I shall give you.

- Take on the identity of a native speaker. This gives you the freedom of the behaviours of the other language – to do things, without embarrassment, that you would not normally do, like waving your arms about.

- Model the teacher, so you get into the physiology of the language: take on all their movements, facial expressions – everything; you will be surprised how much information you pick up.

- Pretend you understand everything: even if you do not at the beginning, you will by the time the speaker has finished – we all repeat ourselves endlessly.

- Say the word in your language, standing in one spot; then move to another spot and say the word in the other language. What differences do you experience? Whereabouts in your body does each word come from? What does each word feel like?

- Have fun!

- Explain to your conscious mind what you are going to do and, as it will undoubtedly get very bored with all the frivolity, ask it if it would like to go off and do something else while you are playing with the other language, knowing that it can come back later, as soon as you need it.

- Remember: you are communicating – everything else is irrelevant.

SCIENCE

The sciences were a dead loss as far as I was concerned: popular culture decreed that one could not do languages and science. It was not until I read *The Tao of Physics* and *The Dancing Wu Li Masters* that I realized that the arts and sciences could not possibly be separated. In the old days one used to ask the question: 'Do you believe in God?' and get the answer: 'Of course not – I'm a scientist.' Nowadays if you ask the same question, you may well get: 'Of course I do – I'm a scientist.'

If my teachers had taught me about slime mould in biology, they really would have grabbed my attention because, for me, slime mould is the most wonderful creation. It is mono- cellular, like the amoeba, and when times are good, each little cell goes about its business and does its own thing. When times are hard, millions of these cells join together and become a slug-like creature that sets off in search of food; this means that only the surface cells are exposed to the rigours of the weather while the millions inside are protected. If this new creature does not discover a supply of food, it becomes something else – this time more like a plant – with a funnel through which spores can escape to be blown on the wind, so that the species will survive. And slime mould is one of the lowest forms of life!

I think what really bored me the most about education was the idea that we had to serve our time doing really useless little things because people imagined that we were not intelligent enough to grasp a bigger concept. Einstein claimed that 'the whole of science is nothing more than a refinement of everyday thinking', and he thought primarily in terms of visual images and feelings, only resorting to words when he needed to express himself. He describes these processes as 'rather vague play', 'combinatory play' and 'associative play', from which we may deduce that he was having a lot of fun. If science is still a closed book to you, remember that there are lots of scientists out there longing to be understood. Science is just a different way of thinking about life, the universe and everything.

MEMORY AND STUDY SKILLS

Peter Russell's *Brain Book* and David Lewis's *Mind Skills* and *The Alpha Plan* are full of information about the mechanics of the brain, and how to make good use of the equipment. Tony Buzan, author of *Use Your Memory* and *Make the Most of Your Mind*, specializes in memory. These books are fun and full of good ideas.

SUPPOSEDLY NOT SERIOUS SUBJECTS

There is plenty to amuse you in the bibliography, especially if you have never had the chance to indulge yourself in any of this sort of non-academic learning or thought you were hopeless at some or all of it. If you consider self-indulgence to be a shocking waste of time, ask yourself whether Leonardo da Vinci would have been a better scientist if he had not been an artist, and whether he would have painted better had he not wasted so much time on science.

If you want to learn to draw, read the books by Betty Edwards. My art mistress wept tears of joy when I gave up drawing at school and I now surprise and delight myself by what I can produce, and know that I could get better and better if I spent more time on it.

Joseph O'Connor, Mickey Hart, Tim Gallwey and Don Campbell will help you to discover new worlds in sound. You can model Mozart using Robert Dilts's monograph, *Wolfgang Amadeus Mozart: Songs from the Spirit*.

On sport, read Tim Gallwey for tennis, skiing and golf; Mary Wanless for riding; Thomas Crum for aikido and John Whitmore for driving and sailing. *Juggling for the Complete Klutz* by John Cassidy and B.C. Rimbeaux is available with balls in toyshops, and the refined Grinder learning-to-juggle method is in *Turtles all the Way Down* by Judith De Lozier and John Grinder.

Pause for Thought:
About our 'Elders and Betters'

Blame is wonderful! It shifts the burden. Adam blamed Eve, and Eve blamed the serpent. If I knew then what I know now … goodness knows what damage I did to my children in moments of irritation, infuriation, exhaustion, etc. But they have survived and taken charge of their own lives. And I wonder what would happen if everyone in the world decided to take responsibility for their own actions, for their own learning, and for their own future.

They do their best, our 'elders and betters'. I believe that parents want the very best for their children and, above all, they do not want their children to make the same mistakes that they made. When babies are born, they are totally vulnerable and have to be protected from the effects of an apparently cold, hard world; and some of us are so conditioned to protect our young that we go on doing it far longer than is good for them – or us, come to that.

My parents are long since dead, but I still expect one or the other to appear and tell me that my latest idea is not a good one because: 'what might people say?'; 'I might find myself in deep water'; 'this could be interpreted as …' – whatever the current 'bogey man' happens to be.

I know now that all this was because they cared; they cared what happened to me. Fine, so it drove me mad at the time, but they were doing their best, according to the limited choices that they had. A Victorian-type upbringing was all they knew: this was the way that things were 'supposed' to be.

And if we think about all those who are set in authority over us; if we think about the feelings of inadequacy that we all suffer from; if we consider how people who care might prepare the new blood for initiation, we can understand ideas like: 'Keep control, otherwise *they* will gain the upper hand.'

Adults realize, consciously or otherwise, that the young can run rings around them. The Law of Requisite Variety in cybernetics (the study of systems) holds that the most flexible part in any system is the one that will survive the longest; and the young know how to be infinitely flexible. *Our 'elders and betters' feel no less inadequate than anybody else* – they need to protect themselves, as much as ordinary mortals like you and I.

Children have a highly developed moral sense; they also have a highly developed sense of discipline. And, while I would agree that their ideas about noise level and expending of energy do not always correspond with ours, I do not believe that any child is wilfully bad. They may do dreadful things, but I suspect that this is either part of their curiosity – of their 'I wonder what would happen if ...' experimental philosophy – or to satisfy an unconscious need to protect themselves, or to make themselves feel better.

As we grow older, we find ourselves more and more hidebound by 'manners'; personal questions are frowned upon, questions our 'elders and betters' cannot answer may be frowned upon, endless 'whys' are frowned upon as 'just being a nuisance'. A teacher of children with insatiable curiosity may well feel discomfort at being asked all these questions, and have a consequent fear that the children are getting the upper hand, and may try to crush this wilfulness before things get out of control.

Mentors, Metaphors and Models

MENTORS

When the young Telemachus went off in search of his father, Ulysses, he was accompanied by Minerva, the goddess of wisdom, who had taken on human form in the shape of his friend Mentor to act as his guide, wise counsellor and faithful friend. We can have all this support for ourselves by creating our own mentors.

The great thing about mentors is that you can keep them in your head, always available whenever you want them. I once allowed myself to be seriously upset by somebody else. Furious with myself for allowing this to happen, I decided to telephone Ian McDermott to ask him to sort me out, but I was too mean to pay for the call, so I conjured him up in my mind. There he was, with his head slightly on one side, smiling gently, shaking his head despairingly and saying, 'Diana, *who* is driving your brain?' And that was it! The problem just disappeared.

As mentors, I always have a horse and a dog available. Which horse it is depends on the resources I need at the time – they all have grace, elegance, strength, kindness and generosity – but sometimes I am in need of extra speed, stamina, courage, humour, fun or flexibility. The dog is one of three beloved flatcoated retrievers. These dogs have no hang-ups: when they want attention, they ask for it; they are always cheerful, specialize in enjoying life, and never really grow up.

For courage, I have Jean-Louis Guntz, an officer of the world famous Cadre Noir (the instructors at the French

Cavalry School, who are the epitome of elegance in their black uniforms – see page 157), riding along beside me. When we lived in France, if I was really lucky, I would meet him out exercising and he would take me under his wing and provide me with endless fun over fences. One day Jean-Louis asked me if I had ever jumped a particularly nasty-looking drop fence off a road, down on to a muddy bank and on downwards into the darkness. When I told him I had not, he said: 'Off you go!' Clearly this was a language problem, so I explained carefully that the reason I had never jumped it was because I did not want to; all he said was: 'Vous allez voir! Vous allez voir!' And of course, it was not nearly as frightening as it looked; having plunged down into the bowels of the earth, we came up the other side and out over a sunken wall into the sunlight. In fact, it was so exhilarating that I took to jumping it when I was on my own, just for fun. Jean-Louis remains beside me to this day, saying: 'You'll see! You'll see!', whenever I do not want to try something just because it looks as though it might be nasty.

On my desk I have a photograph of John Grinder playing the kalimba on the beach in Santa Cruz. John is my lifeline. He is always in my mind when I need him to get me out of trouble and to answer questions.

There is also a picture of Gregory Bateson, whom I never knew, drawn by Robert Dilts. He is available to keep my thinking on track and to remind me of the questions I need to ask. Robert is on my left, with his head slightly on one side, smiling and waiting for me to answer for myself a question I have just asked him. Todd Epstein is either behind me with a hand on my back so I can feel his strength, warmth and laughter, or sitting on a high chair, smiling quietly to himself, looking like the kindliest of wolves, and waiting for just the right moment to drop his bombshell or pearl of wisdom. Todd is my timing mentor. Judith DeLozier just *is* there, *being* herself, because that is who Judy is: she is all about *being*. On my desk there is a picture of a giant redwood, which she sent me. The redwood is a massive tree, which, in spite of its solid trunk, must show the ultimate in flexibility in the way that it grows, protects and propagates itself to become the world's tallest tree and one of the most long-lived.

A client was terrified that he was going mad: he used to talk to his late wife, when he was in doubts about something. I could relate to that immediately, because the late Errol Prior-Palmer (father of Lucinda Green, whom you will meet later) is still very much with me, primarily for his strength, wisdom, laughter and keen sense of the ridiculous, and when I need his help, I have no hesitation in calling on him.

I have Placido Domingo rising to an exquisite high note, which lifts me, mind and body, into a completely different state. The sound of his voice is all that I need but, if I am feeling self-indulgent, I allow myself to see him on his Andalusian horse, riding through the early morning sunshine (a scene from *Cavalleria rusticana*), so I can smell the dew and allow myself to be completely carried away.

Anyone and everyone who has ever existed in fact or fiction is available to you as a mentor, from Shakespeare to Sherlock Holmes. When in doubt, call in a specialist, and you will be amazed by what you learn: walk and talk with Aristotle along the shady paths round the Lyceum; dance with Nureyev or Fonteyn; sing the duet from *The Pearl Fishers* with Domingo; become Laurel or Hardy and see what a fine mess you get into; ride on a light beam with Einstein; draw, paint or invent with Leonardo. Everything is available through the collective consciousness, and all you have to do is to allow whatever you need to be there for you.

You could ask yourself 'What would so-and-so say or do in this situation?' Then step into that person's shoes, like you did in the first modelling experiment when you 'became' somebody else, and discover the answer. Or you could call your mentor on an imaginary telephone and ask him or her questions. Or you could invent something completely different that would be even more effective for you.

METAPHORS

Thinking in metaphor is very useful for reorganizing the muddles we get into by scrambling logical levels of thought; for example, by getting confused between behaviour and identity. As an illustration, I think of people in terms of cats and dogs. I am a dog, and go up to people wagging my tail. Not everybody likes dogs; they can be intimidating, and a large dog wagging its tail at coffee-table height can cause chaos. Being aware of people's reactions to dogs makes me more aware of their reactions to me. Cats, on the other hand, are more self-contained and generally content to sit with their tails round their paws, waiting for someone else to make the overtures. So, if someone does not respond in kind to my enthusiastic tail-wagging, it is not necessarily because they do not like me: when a cat starts to lash its tail, it is time to watch out.

At other times I am Kipling's little elephant with insatiable curiosity, and am well aware that a little elephant is an unusual thing to find in your office or at a party; also, however little, an elephant is very heavy and powerful. And when the little elephant poked his nose into the crocodile's business, the consequences were very painful, although the end result was a wonderfully useful trunk. This metaphor also reminds me that before stepping gaily into unknown territory, I need to make sure that my other three feet are on solid ground.

James Pritchard of The Driving Business trains company-car drivers in how to avoid accidents. He asked me for a metaphor for myself as a driver, and I really had to think. I knew that I saw the road itself as a channel and my route, and everything on it as flowing water. Was I a fish? No, that would not do, because I immediately saw a picture of a trout swimming upstream, which was definitely not me. Eventually we came to the conclusion that I was just water, going with the flow. James wonders how effective the lions, tigers and bulls are when it comes to their own and other people's safety. His training is so effective that insurance companies are now allowing discounts to fleets whose drivers have spent time with him.

Robert Dilts and Todd Epstein developed their metaphor of 'fish' in the training room from Gregory Bateson's study of dolphin training. The dolphins were rewarded for doing something right by the sound of a whistle, and a fish: this was the 'task' fish. From time to time, the trainers would slip the dolphins an unearned fish, without blowing the whistle – a 'relationship' fish. This concept was developed after the dolphins went on strike and refused to do anything, when their training was purely task orientated. Robert and Todd have a 'fishbowl', which is full of different coloured fish pictures: goldfish, starfish, angelfish, swordfish. When someone has done something that you liked, you write the compliment on your chosen fish and give it to them. During our trainers' training course 40 of us got through over 3,000 fish, which means that, on average, every student had 75 permanent reinforcements of things that he or she had done well (in three different systems: something to look at, words, and something to touch).

Metaphors and stories are an excellent way of getting your message across without interfering with someone else's model of the world, of making suggestions without telling the other person what to do. Tell me a story and I can either take it or leave it. The conscious mind likes facts, and it may well consider that paying attention to anything as unsubstantiated as a mere story is beneath its dignity; so it will wander off, leaving the unconscious free to benefit from the message without any outside interference. The unconscious has infinite potential for changing things around to suit itself: although we may not have had a wicked stepmother and two ugly sisters, we can resonate with being treated as drudges, feeling inadequate, going to the ball, meeting a handsome prince or princess, losing track of time and having to rush home.

We can find metaphors everywhere. For example, a cup of tea can be a metaphor for anything from 'you're welcome' to 'come in take the weight off your feet, relax and let's have a chat'.

My metaphor for my conscious mind, left brain, Self 1 is Sir Humphrey Appleby. If you watched *Yes, Prime Minister*, or

Yes, Minister when he was plain Mr Appleby, you will be aware that he rose from being merely an Important Civil Servant to the dizzy heights of Cabinet Secretary and head of the Civil Service. Sir Humphrey has many behaviours, beliefs and values that we may not like, but he did not get to where he is today without being able to organize things properly. Sir Humphrey gets me from A to B on time, organizes my calendar, gets my paperwork done, meets deadlines and arranges meetings with all the right people. There was a time when he would have nothing to do with my unconscious mind because he had not been introduced, and therefore considered my unconscious to be beneath his notice. Now they work brilliantly together – frequently on a 'need to know' basis; in other words, they do not tell me what is going on because they know how bossy I am and that I will probably only interfere. They make such a good team that I am happy to leave them to get on with the day-to-day running of my life.

When I started to learn about NLP, I went to see a local practitioner. As I set off, I had a very sharp pain in my left temple; I enquired what it was about, and there was Sir Humphrey saying that this visit was not a good idea. I promised I would look after him, and the pain went away. When I arrived at my destination, I told the practitioner about Sir Humphrey's worries. He made a squelching, dismissive gesture with his fingers, saying, 'He's just a nobody, a clerk; give him some filing to do and that will keep him quiet.' I was furious! You don't treat a senior civil servant like that, least of all a Cabinet Secretary. I expect every part of my mind to be treated with the utmost respect, care and attention, because I know that they are all working for my best interests – no wonder poor Sir Humphrey had not wanted to go.

Choose metaphors that work for you. Some people hate the electric fence that I have installed for my protection because they do not like the idea of people being zapped. It works for me, as I do not believe that there are many people out there who wish me ill and, if they do, a small electric shock will usefully warn them off and make them think twice about harming anyone else. Some people prefer a bulletproof perspex shield, but that would give me claustrophobia, and cut out the physical contact that I need. Some people like barbed wire; I don't because of the possibility of blood poisoning. Some are the fastest gun in the West, but I could not stand the strain of being in that state of alertness for danger twenty-four hours a day. There are lights, colours, force fields, waterfalls, police dogs: you have infinity to choose from when looking for a metaphor for your protection, and to discover something that works perfectly for you. The trick is to make sure that what you want fits the metaphor, rather than altering the metaphor in some way to suit your needs; then you know that it will really work for you. For example, if I had chosen to be a fish in the flow of traffic, I would be permanently worried about having to swim upstream (causing frustration and aggravation), holding my own against the current (too much like hard work) or being eventually swept out to sea (which was not where I wanted to be).

A friend of mine was working with someone who was driving his colleagues mad with his latest passion: Total Quality Management. 'It's my religion!', he announced proudly. 'Oh,' said Nelda, gently, 'and does that mean you are prepared to die for it?' That one, simple question brought the whole power of the metaphor to bear, and he realized that what he had chosen was not suitable. Now he has something more appropriate, and the company has TQM that they can all enjoy.

When you have chosen something, try it out and see how it works; maybe it is perfect, maybe as you use it you will become aware of more things that you need. You can change it in any way that you like, update it, make it larger or smaller, lighten it up and so on. Or you can choose something completely different until you find what works for you, with all the resources you need. My final metaphor question is 'How do you think of yourself as a learner?' As you know, I am a sea otter, having a lovely time learning through play, or a little elephant with insatiable curiosity. If you are short of ideas, you might like to look through *Medicine Cards* by Jamie Sams and David Carson for inspiration. If you want to choose a living creature, the book will give you lots of ideas.

MODELS

Here is a chance for you to discover for yourself what goes on inside a collection of people whose success appears to stem from particular parts of their learning equipment – Sir John Harvey-Jones is generally described as a visionary, Terence Stamp has become a wizard with words, Lucinda Green succeeds on a horse, Adam Palmer's genius is in the field of taste and smell; David Edwards can do sums in his head – or a combination of two systems: Colin Reeve combines the kinaesthetic world of karate with the cerebral world of management consultancy; Catherine Harman would pursue success in sport and games relentlessly until she got it, combining this with her eye for beauty in architectural salvage; Judith DeLozier has brought her experience from the worlds of dance and anthropology into the technical, structured world of NLP. The only qualification for selection as a model is that each had to have reached the top in their respective fields. David and Judy have degrees; the rest have not got a single academic qualification between them. Terence describes himself as the product of two working-class dynasties, and Colin still thinks of himself as a fifteen-year-old toolmaker.

The object of this exercise is for you to discover the structure of what we, as outsiders, would regard as success. Who these people are and what their field is, are unimportant: you are looking for the structure rather than the content. How do they think about what they want to do? What do they believe about themselves and life in general? What are they doing on the planet? Some of the things that they say may appear complete rubbish to you; the trick here is to ask yourself what changes would happen inside you if you said those sorts of things. I was telling a friend about Colin's Russian dolls, and he said he had never heard such nonsense in his life – the man must be a complete idiot. This friend is so entrenched in his own model of the world that he cannot conceive the possibility that everybody else is not exactly like him. His strategy is to compare the rest of the world with himself and find it wanting, rather than to compare himself to the rest of the world – and learn something. I wonder what you will discover about yourself as you compare and contrast what the models say about themselves with what you see, hear and feel in specific situations.

Arm yourself with a selection of different-coloured highlighter pens, and go on a language hunt using one colour for visual words and expressions, such as *look!*; *let me see*; *clear*; *bright*; *point of view*; *perspective*; another colour for auditory expressions; such as *it sounds ...* ; *listen!*; *it rings a bell*; *harmony*; *music to my ears*; *something tells me*; and another colour for feelings: *smooth*; *soft*; *grasp*; *hold on*; *touch*; *in another person's shoes*; *rough*; *being driven by* or *drawn to something* and so on.

How do the models think about time? Are they orientated towards the past, the present or the future?

How do they think about other people? Is learning a question of 'task' or 'relationship'? How do they think about mistakes? Do they direct their own lives, or do they rely on other people to do that for them?

How much time do they spend in first position: experiencing things from inside themselves? How much are they in second position: seeing things through the other person's eyes? And how much in third: detached from the situation and not involved with either side? A useful pointer for this is the use of 'one' instead of 'I' or 'me', or the sort of formal language that is normally written, rather than spoken, English. If you really want to do a serious job, you can use Robert and Todd's Jungle Gym, which separates the different logical levels, marking out the spaces for time and the different positions that they take.

What have all my models got in common? When you have discovered the patterns, it might be fun to do some modelling yourself – with people who find learning difficult as well, so that you can discover the differences that make the difference between super learners and non-super learners? All you have to do is ask them the same questions as I did at all the different logical levels, paying particular attention to their beliefs about their capabilities.

David Edwards

David is a retired Lloyds underwriter who made money while the rest of the world lost its shirt – by the simple expedient of being an honest man who can do sums.

Where and when he learns

Mornings. Another facet of getting older: I think your brain tires. On the other hand, I was playing quite good bridge at 3.00 am the other night, but that's something that interests one – really probably the deciding factor. Occasionally, one remembers something one was told: a pearl of wisdom happens to stick in one's brain.

Where and when he does not learn

When it's in words I don't understand, I don't attempt to learn. When it is something that bores me, I switch off. As one gets older, another time you switch off is when you only half hear things; as one gets deafer, there is nothing more irritating than getting a tiny bit of a conversation – it's much easier to switch off.

What he learns

I don't think at this age one learns an awful lot. I think one's brain is supposed to reach its zenith at the age of twenty-one, after which your mental powers deteriorate but your experience increases, until you end up about my age: all experience and no brain.

If it interests you, learning is no effort; if it doesn't interest you, I don't think you learn it at all. I learn about the sort of things that interest me. I read a lot: one is always absorbing something from that.

What he does not learn

Everything that bores me. I don't know whether it's idleness or not, but something complicated one finds almost impossible to master as one gets older.

Q. We become more choosy about what we learn?
Oh, yes. We can't be bothered to learn a lot. Whoever wants to learn bureaucratic gobbledygook and things like that? If they can't put it in English, you can't be bothered to read it. I often wonder how much people do understand; or whether they are all a load of pseuds who have just got patter. Their words mean nothing: I look them up and it still doesn't mean anything. I have a theory that most things can be described in simple language and, where it goes outside the simple language, the explainer is either concealing their own ignorance, or trying to confuse you.

David was a classical scholar, and has the root of almost every formal English word in his head, so a bureaucrat who can confuse him, can confuse anybody.

I have a curious mind. Up to a certain point I'd find things like mathematics terribly easy. In advanced mathematics at school I got something like 98 per cent – I just understood it, so it was only a question of writing it down. Then there is a whole higher area of mathematics – almost semi-philosophical – which was, like all philosophy, a complete closed book to me: I didn't understand a word.

Q. How do you know when you have understood something?
I know when I don't because it's just a blank. To understand something, you've got to absorb it and see what it means. If you don't understand it you absorb nothing – unless you are a parrot. The whole thing is a mist and it just disappears out of the window – it's nothing. When I understand something, it all fits into place.
   I have a theory, which I think is probably wholly untrue, that you shouldn't fill your mind up with useless porridge or whatever: it's taking up space that could be used for more

valuable things. It may be – and I half suspect it is – an excuse for not learning the things one doesn't want to learn.

I had very easy schooldays: everything came terribly easily. I was rather bored. I once wrote home from school saying I was bored and got an awful rocket from my mother – a very sensible lady, saying, 'boredom is a habit of mind, and it is entirely up to you not to be bored'.

I had a particularly undistinguished career in the army. It's funny, I always remember my failures, never my successes; I always remember even minor failures other people have never even noticed, but I blame no one but myself.

How he learns

Reading; other people; saying to yourself 'that makes sense – funny I never thought of it before' and remembering it. No conscious effort to remember anything – I just do; going back to first principles; being open-minded; being aware; being honest with yourself; asking the right questions; making up your mind on the evidence – always bearing in mind that you might be wrong.

The more you dig, the harder it is to find reality – especially military history: battles that were not successful, just did not happen. When you meet people you have been in the war with, you remember entirely different things.

How to be open-minded? Question all the time: only the very stupid are very confident and have closed minds. It's all a question of guessing and assessing the odds. I've had things staring me in the face for thirty years that I've always regarded with deep suspicion, largely because I've never taken the trouble to find out about them. You're always dealing with things you don't understand as an underwriter; part of being an underwriter is that you listen to stories, and quite often you change your mind.

How to be aware? I have fairly good antennae; like a cat's whiskers; feeling things, through tone of voice, body language (as they call it), being aware of the feelings of other people.

I had the strong impression, as he described this, of all his senses coming out of him to pick up whatever was in the atmosphere.

Things all spring into my mind [gesture at eye level]; I don't flag them up [upward gesture with right hand]. I can imagine the Battle of Hastings and Waterloo and things. I can be there, taking part. Funnily enough, I don't hear any noise. Smells are the most evocative things. Put me down blindfold, and I can smell Cairo, no trouble at all … Smells are the things, to my mind – more than anything.

These people who meet someone and sum them up in a moment – it's absolute rubbish. People are far more complex than that.

How he knows which questions to ask
Going back to first principles and thinking about it. With a bit of practice in your head, the whole thing just rolls out [this was accompanied by an upward, semicircular gesture which came out at eye level].

I asked him for the factors in two different insurance questions. He visualised both, and then checked his feelings: the one he was certain about felt complete; the other one did not.

How he does not learn

Your previous experience tells you when its nonsense, and you switch off.

Why? His beliefs and values

Above all, the most important of everything in life is honesty. Be honest with yourself – you might be wrong. If one continues to take an interest in things, you automatically read about, listen about, think about things. It's really a question of keeping one's interest – I don't learn about things that don't interest me.

Who?

He is who he is and, with his loathing for philosophy, does not think further than that.

Catherine Harman

Catherine, who worked in architectural salvage, was one of the most interesting people that I have known. She loved a challenge, and once learned all the answers to Trivial Pursuit just for fun. My project with her was never finished. She was killed in a head-on collision in 1993 at the age of thirty-three, so we will never know how she learned all the answers to Trivial Pursuit apart from the fact that she did it in the bath.

When I asked what she was best at, she said, 'Finding things and finding out about things.' She also enjoyed winning and would take something up simply in order to win: backgammon, clay pigeon shooting, golf – and once she had got to the top, she might well have got bored and given it up. Golf remained a ruling passion.

On winning

The only way to win is to practise and work hard at it. You don't win all the time, but you play to win. You can't win all the time, because you will always find somebody better than yourself. You don't play any game without wanting to win, because otherwise what's the point of playing? You must win legally, you mustn't cheat. You have to win purely through merit – because you are better than somebody else on the day.

I would never win at things I am not interested in. If you think you can do it entirely by yourself, you're wrong. Failure is failure to yourself – I couldn't give a toss about anybody else. Winning isn't the end-all and be-all. Winning is knowledge to a certain extent. All knowledge is good; winning makes you feel good. It's much cooler to be potentially brilliant than brilliant. It's more entertaining. What else are you going to do, once you've got the game licked?

Where and when she learned

Life is learning. It depends on the people you are with. If you don't have the connection, you don't learn so much. You learn more when you feel secure in yourself.

Where and when she did not learn

When I'm bored.

What she learned

Everything that is interesting or useful. You can gather from other people's strengths and knowledge from watching them, especially in sport.

What she did not learn

What I don't want to learn or am not interested in; what is unnecessary, unimportant, a waste of time: I can spend that time doing something more interesting.

How she learned

Always surrounding myself with people who know what they

are doing: you'll never learn unless you learn from others – if you don't have connection with people, you don't learn much; being open-minded and being able to listen to others objectively. Reading a lot – it's another point of view; looking things up; trial and error: one of the best ways to learn is through mistakes.

By watching. You learn to speak through hearing and watching. Watch and then imitate or copy what the other person is doing. Once you have copied something, if you then consider it is what you wanted to copy, I think it then becomes filed by picture. I can hit a golf ball like Faldo. It would look good and it would feel good.

How to watch
Be able to interpret what you see. You can see the world differently every day – it depends on what you're feeling inside. When my mind is here, in learning mode, I'm building memories: creating the scene; imagining myself there. For golf, I take a photograph in my mind's eye.

Her internal pictures were in different places and of different quality, depending on the ability and stature of the golfer she was thinking of.

How she learned from her mistakes
I step out and look where I'm going wrong. I stand away and think about it. In golf, the more you worry about it, the stiffer you become, and the less likely you are to hit the ball.

What was going on inside her when she was learning
I feel fascinated. It feels exciting: butterflies up in the stomach and chest. The whole outlook on life is different: the world all looks rosy.

How she listened
You have to have an interest in what they are saying. I am either awake or asleep, and sometimes my mind is elsewhere, and I just don't hear.

How she remembered
Replaying the tape in my head [looking over to her left], and constructing pictures. The smell of money brings it all very clear; it's a different sense, you don't physically smell it, but you have a feeling, so you retain it.

How to be open-minded
Listen to other people's opinions. It all goes back to self-confidence: you can't have self-confidence, you cannot be open-minded unless you have an opinion of your own; and you can only have an opinion of your own if you have thought about it. If you know what you believe you can relate other people's opinions to it, putting yourself in their shoes, feeling what is going on inside them.

How she did not learn

Boredom! I switch off. I see doom and gloom pictures [black and white, slightly off to the left]. It's like being in a cage – just sort of trapped – you can't get away. There are no sounds. There's a feeling of cloudiness in my head [left hand from shoulder downwards]. When I'm really bored, I go to sleep and, hopefully, when I wake up, it will be less boring. It comes through my body: I suddenly feel terribly tired and I just go out cold – I can do that anywhere.

Why she did not learn

I have a very low boredom/concentration level.

Adam Palmer

Friends refuse to eat with me at Champneys, the health resort: they have put themselves on diets, while I am there for the food. Adam is twenty-eight, and he became Champneys'

Maître de Cuisine in 1989. He is very aware of how he pro-cesses things, and his language demonstrates how he uses all his senses to code and retrieve information.

When he learns

I'm awful in the mornings – I get good at about five o'clock at night.

When he does not learn

I don't learn anything when I have pressures from outside. I have to be totally dedicated to one thing.

The day to day running of the kitchen consists of ordering and organizing people. If you come in with a positive attitude and no pressure on you, you know that what you can create that day will be good if you put effort into it. But if one extra thing crops up, I start thinking ahead: I have to have every-thing organised and *mise en place* (probably one of the most important things that you are taught at college, this means 'everything in its place') – getting ready for the next service. If I can't see everything laid out in a line by a certain time, then I probably start to feel 'we're going to be up the wall tonight'. You work on time limits all the time: if that isn't done, you won't be able to do that, and you won't be able to do that. It is a big chain, and you look along it and, the further you look along the chain, the darker it gets, and you're going: 'it's not going to work today!', and you slip down that ladder and you think you've got to do something. You slip down the ladder if you don't get a grip of yourself. It also depends on everybody else's mood, because we are very much a team.

The future? Out in front. But only to the limit of one day when I'm cooking. I might touch on tomorrow's menu in the morning and just whack it in the back of the head (gesture to the right base of the head). To get the best out of myself, I've just got to be totally dedicated to that day.

The past? I might think about something that I know I can improve. It goes back a couple of weeks but, after that, everything becomes very blurry, because we are moving on all the time. We've all done things that we regret, and we remember those. They make me chuckle now; they are probably the only things that really stick in my mind. It's great: that is the best way of learning.

Where he learns

The learning I do at home is improvization – you create some wonderful things. I wanted to roast some parsnips; I opened the cupboard and a pot of English mustard fell out, and I thought 'mustard and parsnips would probably go quite well. We'll do mustard and honey and roast the parsnips' – and it's just the best thing! I come across things totally by accident. It's a great way of learning. Bring it into a professional situation with fifty people saying it's wonderful – that's good!

I learn more at work, because I am really keyed into it: there are too many distractions at home. At work, it doesn't matter if you mess it up. You are not cooking because you're hungry: if you are just cooking to create something, it doesn't matter if it doesn't work. I miss learning from other chefs; I feel that most of the stuff in the kitchen is coming from me, although it's a very open kitchen – everyone is involved because I think it's good for people. I have learned things from the dietician that I never learned before.

When I thought I had learned as much as I possibly could, I began to lose interest a little bit. Food really wasn't important here: it was a facility. I have been taught that the kitchen is the most disciplined area of a hotel. It was much more relaxed here than I was used to. Mark (the chef when I came here as *sous chef*) taught me that there is a lot more to life than work. I can't thank him enough for that. We give people two days off a week together now, which is totally unheard of in this business. I think it is so important, if people are working that hard ... at the end of the day, the place will still be here on Monday, it will still run.

My team are much more dedicated than when I first came here; they feel very passionately about working in a decent establishment and cooking what they perceive as decent food, but I think that they would much rather look at it than eat it. People think that it must be good, because it looks good. People come for interviews and they say the food looks good; I tell them it tastes good as well. When they write a menu, before they ever look at taste combinations, they look at colour combinations; it's very important, but it must run in line with what you are doing taste-wise. I think that glossy books and magazines have created glossy food.

I wasn't born with that amount of artistry – I just created it. How? All it is, is experience: it's all a matter of balance. Having odd numbers of pieces of garnish looks a lot nicer than having even numbers. In nature, things grow unevenly – that's why we have big bits of chervil; if it's looking alive, it looks fresh and you want to eat it.

Where he does not learn

When I don't see the necessity for it. I wasn't very interested at school. I just wanted to get out and do what I wanted. I don't think of myself as using my brain all day: writing the book was a nightmare.

What he learns

How to deal with people: I used to find it a problem meeting guests, and giving chef's demonstrations. Now I enjoy it; I get to meet interesting people, to get a bit of a buzz. I know how to deal with it when I'm bored now. It's just a confidence thing. My demos are really informal. I think chefs are scary to people. I get down to their level and, if I can't answer their question, I tell them. I don't know everything.

How he learns

Questioning accepted facts; adapting information to my situation. I probably draw a little mental picture a lot of the time.

How he does not learn

When I'm bored, something kicks in my brain: 'we've been here before; we've done all this before', a voice, then I start to lose it: everything goes sort of blank, when you don't have any interest and you can't see anything wonderful happening from the next move you are going to make, you can't see any future in it.

I told him he'd got to go on a training course on accountancy tomorrow.

I start thinking about what I've got to do tomorrow in the kitchen, as soon as you say this, because that doesn't interest me. There's something in the back of my mind saying: 'yes, this is going to be useful because, if I ever decide to have my own business, this will be awfully useful'; there's another thing in the back of my mind saying: 'but it's not awfully relevant'. In the training course situation, my concentration goes in about ten-minute bursts. I will make the effort: I'm totally into everything I do. It's a classroom situation and I always draw some similarities. I like to keep things rolling all the time and, if it is not flowing, that's when I lose it.

Why he learns

I think this job is unique: if you were the best cook in the world, you would not necessarily be good at Champneys. I think it's good to have rapport with the guests: I think it's good to have it anywhere, if you want to be successful. If someone wants a well-done steak, that's what he wants. I can deal with it better now; that comes with maturity.

What, all of a sudden makes you an authority when you become a parent? That's always what confuses me. Different situations arise: situations that kids are in today that I wasn't in, and they are probably more qualified to answer the questions than I am. I can tell them why I think that they shouldn't be doing it, but they need to express their view, and why they think it's right.

Why do I learn? As you get older, you enjoy learning more, because you are not under pressure. I don't think you can ever learn enough about anything. My love of food has only developed over the past five years: I've always enjoyed it and got a lot out of it; but I think you just develop the understanding and enjoyment. I adore what I do, and I would not change it for the world, but I wish I had time to do other things as well; to read more. I try to fit too much into my life, because I don't want to feel that I am missing out on anything.

How he knows the right questions to ask

I turn it round in my mind the whole time. I take it up every possible avenue and if it all comes down on to the same road, then I know. I use everything I know about the subject, push it along these roads, and if it comes down in exactly the same place, or near enough the same place, then I know.

Adam developed this strategy as a result of being laughed at at school, and laughing at other children, who asked questions that they had not thought through.

I love people asking questions, and I love giving the information that I know: I love passing that on.

Why he does not learn

Either because I am not interested or because I think I know
better: there are very few things that I think I know better. I
hate fiction: I admire the imagination but it does not stimu-
late me. I'd much rather read an autobiography: it's real – I
can relate to it.

Who?

I'm getting to be what I want to be in life. I'm just becoming
who I want to be. Back to this confidence thing again. You
have enough confidence to carry something through. You can
air your opinion and stand your ground. I am getting to be the
sort of person that I like, most of the time. If work overtakes
my life, there will always be somebody saying: 'hold on!' I am
always going to have to enjoy what I am doing. It's great, my
job; I love it! And I want to carry on loving it. I can't see into
the future – maybe something different will get me kicking in
ten years' time.

Who else?

My job is very self-motivated. I know that I can always do
more; if I want to do more, I have to do it myself. We wouldn't
have got as far as we have got now without me pushing
people and pushing myself. Food versus paperwork: I just
decided to grab the bull by the horns and say this is my food
now: all the extra pressure isn't going to make the food taste
any better and that is what I'm here for. The more I got
involved, the more I thought: 'This is what I'm here for; this is
what it's all about.' Everybody here could be like robots and
we could be just like a big industrial caterer: it wasn't me, and
it wasn't Champneys.

Lucinda Green, MBE

*We disagreed about how I was to introduce her. I believe that
she is the finest horsewoman that Britain has ever produced.
Lucinda immediately listed all the things that she could not do
to her satisfaction. I have always considered her a child of the
universe: she would tell me about riding with the wind in her
hair and the stars in her eyes, as we sat on our horses by a river,
watching the water rats busying themselves with their daily
lives. She has the most extraordinary communication abilities,
and it is her ability to communicate with horses that has taken
her to the top in three-day eventing (dressage, cross country
and show jumping): she has won Badminton Horse Trials on
six different horses, has been World Champion, and European
Champion twice, and has written several books.*

When she learns

I think that, if your ears are open, you are absorbing things
most of the time. You can learn something from everybody.

When she does not learn

When your eyes are shut and your ears are shut and you are so
busy thinking about what you think is right, and you don't
realize that there's another perception to it, or another side
to it.

Lucinda left school at fifteen with no qualifications.

I was stagnated: I could not move forwards or backwards.
The whole system had only one effect on me: complete turn
off. My mother took me away. From that moment onwards, it

was all flying, wings flapping. I got to an age where I needed to be able to open my wings, and I simply couldn't [holding herself down]. Thirteen, fourteen, fifteen is the age of initiation, and it's when most people in the Western world are absolutely unable to blossom out, because the schooling system prevents it. It was the most extraordinary feeling. I have never been so driven since then by something I was completely out of control of. It was very much an alone thing: a world that was not there for the taking, and as soon as I left school, it was there.

Where she learns

You can learn something about anything at any time.

Where she does not learn

If I'm doing something mundane – I can only think of one thing at once.

What she learns

General knowledge is a little knowledge about an awful lot. I've got so much left that I still have to learn.

I find it incredibly difficult to understand if somebody is trying to tell me the workings of a certain mathematical thing, or the workings of a system: any sort of business set up. They are just talking, and I am forgetting. I hate not knowing how things work. If I could understand, I'd have a lot more confidence, because I would like to know about other things apart from horses. I try to learn things that bore me, if they are necessary – like how the washing machine works. I'm very undisciplined about things that don't interest me – I don't bother about them.

I just like knowing how things run, it would be much easier

if someone drew me pictures of how business systems worked. Reading words would not be so easy. If they could put me in the system, so I could experience how it worked, that would be absolutely wonderful.

If someone was telling me something about horses, I would visualize it straightaway: I'd see it exactly. All the things I have ever done on a horse have been visualized before I've done them: a little film strip running through my mind, which gives my instinct a warm-up, so that when things go wrong, it knows how to react. I'm watching myself in the film strip; I'm not exactly feeling what's going on – I don't have to. Sometimes I'm on the horse, sometimes I'm watching him.

How she learns

I try to attach information to other things that I remember: hang it on some hook, so that I will remember it.

How to ask all the right questions
Walking a course, thinking of all the things that can go wrong: it isn't quite one, two, three; it isn't quite Adam's roads coming in – it's somewhere in between. It's more numbers – of things that can go wrong, and seeing the thing going wrong. I like to be structured, sitting down and organizing things. I love things to be neatly in their place: bricks (the same colour as the house) – structured; everything is right. How does it fit? How can it fit because you have missed out a whole chunk there? But I might not be sure – I might think it is just me being stupid and missing something.

How she does not learn

If it isn't something that I understand, I switch off: I lose the thread. When you've lost the thread, you've got nothing to keep you going, so everything just goes like that [circular hand movement round her face at eye level], and you don't see it clearly any more – there are no pictures being produced: you blank it. Figures immediately make me loose my nerve, because I know that I am not going to understand them. The pictures stop appearing and I am lost.

Why she learns

Basically, I am just interested. I am interested in how grass grows – why should it? I think the whole of creation is amazing: the fear of missing it because you take it all for granted. So it's fun to stop and work it out.

Why she does not learn

It's a retention question; and, also, I am too busy not concentrating on what I am doing, but thinking about what I'm going to do next, or how I've got to get up and do something else – so you don't give yourself time to learn.

Who?

I might have been a horse, but not any longer (it's very easy to climb inside their heads). My child imagination was not held by Alice, or Winnie the Pooh, because it was not factual enough: they didn't make any sense; they weren't real. Fantasizing is all right to a degree, because it lightens things up a bit; but what's real is what matters, and that is what you have got to learn to live with. What is real? I need stories I can relate to. But there is a story that I love: this boy's mother refuses to believe that her son has found a dragon in the house, until it gets so big that it carries the house away on its back. When the mother admits that it exists, it goes back to its original size (of a cat), and the moral is: 'Don't try and blank out on things you don't understand or believe.'

Who else?

I have always been aware that there must be some incredibly good reason to be here, or I wouldn't have been thrown so much success and luck – so out of the ordinary, and so beyond my understanding of what I can do. And therefore I just concluded, well there's obviously something I have got to be doing with all this; there is some reason for this ridiculous amount of stuff happening to someone who really doesn't deserve it; any more than people who work five times harder and just don't get the luck. So I am just interested to see what it is.

Q. Why don't you deserve it?
Because it was done just for me. I wanted the kick. Winning gold medals and all that is great, but the next day you forget about it – it's gone. Winning lasts as long as the day, really. There has got to be more to life than winning. There's nothing like that Union Jack going up the flagpole! But, it's a selfish existence.

I would rather not stay teaching cross country for the rest of my life, but I have to earn a living. I've no doubt I'll find the next thing. I definitely have some gift of communication and some way of giving confidence to people – and for that I am extremely grateful. That is the talent I am using at the moment; I think that is the beginning of what will develop into some more profound help to people.

Q. How did you learn all those communication skills?
That was natural. I just always had it. But there's only ever a percentage that you succeed with – I would not ever say that I can get something into everybody. I believe that you are blessed with certain talents that you either make something of, or they die. I don't know how you create the communication – it's the biggest failing of mankind, isn't it?

Q. What do you do?
For a start, you keep thinking about what the other person is feeling; you put yourself in their shoes, and think 'how would I feel?' That's probably the most important bit.

Bring them out of themselves; give them confidence, by making them feel at ease; by getting them to talk – letting them hold the floor with a subject they can flow about; every now and again offering some sort of olive branch which they can consider, hang on to, and think about. Teaching too is a conversation.

Some people like being looked at; some people don't. I like to look at somebody if I want to see what they are thinking; if I am talking to an interviewer, I will never look at them: I can only think of what I am going to say if I haven't got your eyes which are giving me other messages. It's the picture again: I'm trying to find the answer, and see the answer before I tell you – a human face puts my pictures off. I like eye contact but, at the moment, I'm not trying to read you – I'm trying to read me.

This is a very important piece of information: eyeball to eyeball confrontation with a person in visual mode will get you nowhere – if they cannot see their pictures, they are lost.

You learn a lot by looking at people; that's why I hate teaching people with dark glasses on – I can't see what they're thinking.

Basically, I like people – that's probably a good start. Every time I sit down with anybody, it's a positive vibration; if you cross swords somewhere along the way, then that's a shame. Everybody's got something to teach you. Listen to everybody. Don't ever think you know it all.

My Epitaph? The ability to communicate with my horse which, in turn brought his confidence out as strongly as it could be brought out, to produce his greatest ability. Some incalculable ability I seem to have to stay somehow in balance, which also gives him his confidence. I can understand how a horse feels, and how he is best or when he is not right, which is a feel. I can keep a horse in his best balance, which accentuates the confidence that the communication is giving him. I put myself in his head. I will walk a course through the eyes of my horse: what's he going to think? He's going to come round this corner, and he's never seen anything looking like that ...

Confidence and balance are the two greatest
words in the dictionary

If everything is going in harmony together, then it's like a
beam coming down from the sun, or a spotlight going up.

Life is one big game of confidence: confidence and balance
are the two greatest words in the dictionary and, in my view,
the reason for friendship is to give people confidence; I think
that's what we can do for people, and then they can start to
fly. But, some of the greatest talents of our time are so great
because they have been driven by a feeling of inadequacy – so
how much self-confidence do you want to give people? And
would it extinguish talent?

Colin Reeve

---

*Colin is an international management consultant; he also cre-
ated the Shotokai Foundation and teaches karate-do around
the world, using NLP to enhance the learning process.*

*When he was young he had a brilliant glimpse of the blind-
ing obvious, which goes a step further than my saying we are
all unique. He realized that, if he was unique, he must be
perfect because there was nothing to be measured against.*

Where and when he learns

I learn all the time. For example, I might read one line in a
book, and I'll shut the book, unable to read any more because
I have learned so much from that one line: it's as if everything
I have learned before that is rearranged because of that new
piece of information; then I dream about it for ages, and a
whole lot of new learning takes place. I take it forwards into
the future, to see what is possible now that I know this: I
imagine it in pictures; then I check the picture against what it
feels like and, if it doesn't feel right, I change the picture until
the feelings come right.

Some things come from nowhere. I explain things or draw
them on the board, and I say to myself 'Where's this coming
from?' They are often the best explanations I have ever seen
or heard. I do not know what I am writing on the board; I'm
just writing it.

I learn from feedback, from the clues and cues I get from
other people. When I'm doing something well, I'm hearing
myself doing it. I am talking to myself and saying: 'You're
really doing this well'. I don't have any negative internal dialogue: I know when things aren't as good as they could be
because I don't have this conversation with myself. Also, I
always review what I have done.

I don't separate work and karate. I will have an experience in karate which changes tomorrow's management consultancy. I left school when I was fifteen, and people ask me how come I own my own company, how come I am a management consultant for all these great British companies? I think that karate has become a metaphor for all my learning: a metaphor for life. I was able to learn things through karate that I did not learn in the classroom. The strength that I had was to be able to transfer the learning, which would be primarily kinaesthetic, into all sorts of conceptual and intellectual things.

After I had been practising karate for a long time, wherever I went, I always went with tremendous confidence and, even though I hadn't studied anything about management, I knew that I was not going to have a problem with it. I spent twenty-seven years with this Japanese teacher, and he was a very hard taskmaster intellectually: he was constantly pushing the conversation into intellectual areas, so I was pushing myself through the physical side to be able to stay with him intellectually. I have other friends who, in karate terms, have practised to the same level as I have and yet there is no sign of it in any other side of their life. Our grading criteria for 5th Dan (which I wrote) says: 'must be seen in everything he says and does', the ability to generalize and transfer everything across.

I make more pictures now than I have ever done. With a bit of ambiguous information, I can see immediately where it fits and explode it into something really big because I am looking at the whole picture. That little bit of information is down there [bottom left, being twiddled with his fingers, while he is delineating a large picture in front of him], and I can see the result of that bit of information on the whole picture. When I work with some directors in British industry, it is as if they have got the same bit of information as me, but they don't know where to fit it in the jigsaw.

Asked where and when he did not learn, Colin was unable to answer such a strange question.

What he learns

Specific bits of information which are all leading back to me
and making me richer. There has to be a context of why I
should know something. I'm trying to learn something to add
value to the world – it sounds so pompous!

What he doesn't learn

Anything that's not going towards my outcome. I want to
become the best management consultant in the world. I actually
want to become more than that – I want to be wise; I want to
have wisdom – whatever that is (this sounds pompous again).

How he learns

First I do something and then I reflect on it. I think about the
response that it had and so on. This is the way that I always
believed that I did learn – practical, kinaesthetic: go in and do
something, and see what happens; but that is now absolutely
balanced with intellectually reading or listening to something
and then generalizing it. When I'm learning kinaesthetically,
it's in the instant, in the moment, it's there; it doesn't have the
same power, because I don't generalize it at that point.

*Colin believes that if his neurology is properly wired, he can-
not fail to learn. To prepare himself, he stands up and does a little
bounce on his heels, which settles everything into working order.*

How he does not learn

I said that he really ought to learn how to do his tax return.

Bad picture! I can't hear you. I know you're talking. I'm
hearing all your words, but I'm not listening to you – I'm

listening to me saying: 'I'm not interested'. It's like a Russian doll, when you have another doll inside the doll: there's me inside here in the real world, and there's you out there, trying to get in – taunting us about these tax returns – and I'm not going to let you in. I'm inside here, protected from you. In one ear and out the other is almost exactly the right explanation; I'm just not allowing your words to come in any deeper.

The easier I make my life, the more people want me. Every time I try not to work, they want me to work. It's a real paradox. The reason that people don't succeed is that they haven't realized the paradox: if you want to hurt somebody with a punch, hit them as softly as possible. People don't learn that paradox – they try all their life to hit hard, and it never works. If you want your children to stay close to you: let them go. If you want your managers always to be under your control: give them responsibility. Once you have learned the paradox, life's a real piece of cake.

It's a really hard message in British industry, who are measuring every day by their output, by how much profit they've made; it's a message they are keen to learn. People make figures, figures don't make people; and therefore I work with the key bit, which is the people. You go to these management conferences and they show you the results; they don't tell you about the people who achieved those results and yet those results did not make the people. Change the people and you'll get different results; change those figures and you won't change the people.

Why he learns

I want to be better at what I do; and it's about this mission to try to add value to the world. The sub-mission is to change British industry so it becomes really, really effective and gets the best out of people. More than that, I'm hoping to add value to the lives of the people around me.

I've got three different mentors: the lion, the owl and the oak tree – courage, wisdom and foundation strength, stability and growth. So I measure decisions by those sometimes. What would the lion do? What would the owl do? What would the oak tree do? But the other, overriding one I've got is Peter Pan. Wanting to have fun. I really think it's important to laugh and learn at the same time; in fact I'm not sure you can do it any other way.

I have seen people moving in to attack Colin, and simply falling over before they get anywhere near him.

When I'm in this state of knocking people down without touching them, I'm in contact with everybody in the room, and it's clear to me that I'm in contact with the person I'm doing it with – in the nicest possible sense: they laugh when they fall down. I feel extraordinarily in touch with the earth: I don't think you could lift me up – and yet at the same time light, and able to move anywhere I want: a tremendous connection, with an extraordinary sense of balance.

When people talk about disassociation, association and rapport, I see them all on the same line. If I am disassociated: out of myself, looking at myself, staying away from you; the next level would be associated: in here, in my body, having a conversation with you; but I can go further along the line and extend this sense of self into you – which I would say was rapport: super-association – associated and extending it to you. And the guy who is attacking you: he can't think without you knowing.

We use all the wrong terminology: we have taken something which is a natural process and turned it on its head and said: 'Let's make not learning natural, and learning unnatural. And let's make sure that everybody knows it's hard to learn.' Thinking about phobias: your body, in that fraction of a second, learned to have that reaction over and over again for the rest of your life; and yet, if you're learning to play golf, you might have to swing that club a thousand times before you learn to do it the same way twice. The underlying belief that you are a natural learner has gone.

Why he does not learn

Its about being discerning in what I learn in order to get to where I want to be.

Who?

The answer that comes up is a knight; a knight in shining armour with a white horse – the whole stuff – wandering around to save the maiden in distress, who's industry or whatever. Someone said, if you study one thing enough, you'll learn everything about everything. The content is the same; the context is different. The learning transfers to everything.

Who else?

In relation to his family
It comes out as 'Protector' – not in the autocratic sense, but in the sense of being part of it.

In relation to friends and colleagues
A resource. I want to have fun with them as well. It is important for them to know not to listen to me all the time; what I say this year might be different next year, because I have learned something new.

In relation to the planet
It feels as if I'm an influential part of it; I am playing an important role. There's something more there; I'm a leader, in some way.

In relation to the universe
It's the same: protector, caretaker – again, not in an autocratic sense. There's a lot to learn to be one of them. Have I got time to learn enough?

Sir John Harvey-Jones, MBE

Sir John joined Imperial Chemical Industries (ICI) after an eventful naval career. Under his chairmanship, Britain's largest company changed and grew from its disastrous slump in the 1970s to triumphant profits and re-emergence as one of the country's most successful and best-run companies. Sir John was voted Britain's most impressive industrialist by his peers for three years running. Now retired, he is referred to as the 'business guru'. His books have been translated and sold round the world, and his television series, Troubleshooter, *has been shown to wide acclaim in Britain, Australia and New Zealand.*

I first met Sir John at a seminar. Under his chairmanship, the first half of the day sparkled: when anybody started to whirl off into the abstract, he would ask a friendly question that we could all relate to and bring the discussion back down to the level of ordinary mortals. He had to leave before lunch and, from that moment on, the whole event disintegrated; all that remains in my memory was the nightmare of a learned gentleman reading a brain-numbing paper, the contents of which were a mystery, although the length was unforgettable.

In my quest for excellence, I drove home asking myself 'What were the differences that made the difference between getting the message across and not getting it across?' and these were the conclusions I came to: the 'What's' come from my observation; the rest is mind-reading.

Q. Who is Britain's leading industrialist, Sir John Harvey-Jones?

A. One of us. An ordinary mortal, in tune with other ordinary mortals.

Q. Why is he one of us?

A. He believes himself to be part of the human system. He is interested in everybody and everything. He believes life is fun. We feel safe with him – he is no threat to us.

Q. How does he demonstrate this?

A. He develops rapport at identity level – I'm OK/You're OK. He acknowledges people's beliefs and values. He is open. He learns from every experience. He has fun.

Q. What does he do?

A. He looks at people, he listens, and he matches the rhythm of their breathing, their movements, and their voices. He tells stories to illustrate his points. He uses words to conjure up pictures, sounds and feelings in his listeners so everybody can connect with what he is saying. His offerings are subjective: in his experience. This leaves us the choice of accepting or rejecting them. He laughs and jokes – generally at his own expense.

I bought his book *Making it Happen* in order to check out my mind-reading and to find out more about this extraordinary man. Years later I was watching him on the television, revisiting old friends, and I said, 'How on earth did he learn to do all that?' meaning all those communication skills that people pay fortunes to learn. My husband said, 'Because he knows all the answers'. This raised the next question, 'How did he learn all the answers?' and I realized that he would be the perfect model for this book.

He wanted to help, but his lifestyle is such that time was short; so I decided to concentrate on his beliefs and values, his internal state, his communication skills and his strategy for asking the right questions.

One of the first things people learn at 'rapport school' is to match or mirror the other person's movements because, if the physiology is in tune, the minds can be on the same wavelength. If you watch old friends deep in conversation, you will see that their physiologies are remarkably alike; alternatively, if you are sitting back and relaxed and I am standing over you with my arms folded, telling you all sorts of things that I think you ought to do, you are unlikely to be very receptive. Sir John and I sat down facing each other across the coffee table and I noticed almost immediately that we were both sitting sideways with our legs crossed and one arm along the back of the sofa. I did not ask whether he had done it deliberately; but I feel sure that he steps automatically into the other person's model of the world, without thinking about it. The result was that I immediately felt comfortable and at ease with him, as he began to tell me about his theory that British education programmes people for failure.

For him, Prep School was a nightmare: he was brought up in India until he was seven, when he suddenly found himself abandoned by his parents at this awful place in England. He had nothing in common with the other boys, whose parents turned up in Rolls Royces at week-ends to take them out. Because he was 'different', the other boys gave him a really hard time; so, to get away from them and, because he was determined not to have problems from the staff as well, he immersed himself in school work. He had only one friend, who was 'a bit of a swot', so work would have added to this relationship. For me, the important thing at this stage of his life is that he accepts his part in the way the other boys treated him, 'I was a bit of a wimp', instead of shifting the blame onto them – in other words, he has taken charge of his own brain.

The next step was a crammer, who specialized in getting boys into Dartmouth College where the education was completely focused upon the Navy. 'In history, we learned all about Naval battles, but not a word about the Industrial Revolution; we learned trigonometry but no calculus. I consider myself completely uneducated; I have no qualifications of any sort.' This led on to my theories about feelings of inadequacy, and I was not completely surprised to discover that even England's greatest industrialist suffers from these, just like the rest of us. He believes that his lack of qualifications may be why he has a passion for learning, and for improving himself.

During his time at ICI he went on as many courses as he could and now, even though he is probably busier than he ever was, he still takes up something new every year. One of his new occupations is as chairman of the governors of my old school, where the philosophy now is: 'If you send us your daughter, we will discover her talents and allow her to develop them'. He believes that a teacher's job is not to teach people, but to arrange a situation where they can learn, and that learning will not take place unless there is a wish to learn. He also believes that we learn best from a combination of practice and theory.

He loves learning about and doing completely different things: ICI was quite different from the Navy; his present numerous activities have created a life quite different from that in ICI.

He believes that being British programmes us for failure: being better than anybody else is frowned upon, and anyway we do not deserve to succeed. But he did add that other races have their own peculiar hang-ups.

Friendship is *very* precious to him: once given, you stick to it through thick and thin. Coffee was brought by a waiter who was clearly an old friend; he refused a tip, and I got the impression that this was because one does not take tips from friends. He knows all the staff at his hotel, and all about their families, and they come and talk to him about all sorts of things.

I asked whether life as a submariner had created the learning situation for his communication skills. While he denies that his communication skills are in any way out of the ordinary, he told me a bit about life in a submarine with a crew of forty-two, each of whom was perfectly capable of sinking the ship; about how everyone was down to their underpants (or less) in hot climates, so there were no badges of rank; about the closeness of cramped quarters; about getting to know each other really well; about discovering that everyone had their own individual talents, and their own contributions to make, regardless of rank; and the realization that we are all the same underneath the veneer.

He went on to discuss his surprise when, working in the Cabinet Office, he discovered that his heroes had feet of clay – just like everybody else.

He remains bewildered by, and ill at ease with, people who give the impression that they think they are different: that they are superior to the rest of us, while I wondered whether this impression of superiority was simply a cover for severe feelings of inadequacy.

Physical courage does not seem very difficult but moral courage is, for him, the hardest thing of all. Sadly, there was not time to explore this further, but I was reminded of all the times I had not stood up for the things that I believed in, because my internal state decided that I could not face it.

He believes that, if I ask him a question, it is his duty to answer it as fully as he can with the knowledge available to him. For this reason, he thinks that he may be considered too blunt by many people but, for him, the importance of communication is that it be precise: that the person he is talking to is fully aware of where he is coming from.

His wife tells him he is arrogant – her observations come from a refusal, on his part, to compromise on who he is and what he believes. He has done a lot of work on the parts of himself that he does not like, and feels that, if he went against what he believes, and the person he has now become, he would lose what he has gained. The warrior part of him knows that, while there is always the possibility that he could be wrong, nonetheless he must stand up and be counted when it comes to something that he passionately believes in.

I believe that this is a crucial component of his skill as a communicator. His whole neurology matches what he is saying; and, because we are getting no mixed messages, we feel that we can accept what he says as a different way of looking at things, even though it may be contrary to our beliefs. Whereas, if I am trying to sell you what I know to be a useless piece of equipment, although my words may be convincing, you will unconsciously pick up the more truthful messages that are coming from my body, and – although you may not know why – you will not want to buy it.

He is not happy without eye contact; he feels that something is wrong 'if you are going round the shop floor and you get no eye contact, you know you are sunk'. Listening is another part of the courtesy you pay to other people: how else can you know precisely where they are coming from? The *feeling* of connection is, for him, very powerful: he illustrated this as though he were holding a small ball in his cupped hand at the level of his heart, his fingers pointing in my direction, and turning it slightly by way of adjustment. He said that it came from his soft heart, his astral heart, 'It's intuition; you just feel that everything is right'.

For him, communication must include emotion – not something the Brits are noted for. And emotion means being able to express your feelings about the other person.

It takes time to discover people's strategies for not learning, so I told him about Colin Reeve's Russian dolls. He was able to relate to that at once and became aware of situations where he had stopped himself from learning.

His strategy for knowing how to ask all the right questions is a combination of visual images and feelings: on the evidence that he has, he follows a prognosis, 'If I get the feeling in the shop floor that the manager doesn't actually know what is going on in detail, I'll find ways of testing that, and testing whether reality is different to his perception: by asking, and by looking and by asking to visit, and so on' [while he was saying this, he was looking up at the picture's in his mind's eye, running his right hand along a line parallel to the ground, at chest height – as he followed his prognosis – and then moving that hand round in the testing area, which was below the prognosis line]. 'In reality, in life, things have to be a seamless coat, and you are looking for the bit that juts out. The bit that isn't a part of the seamless coat tells you that there is something else: that that theory is not right. And, until the thing makes a consistent and coherent pattern without jagged edges, it won't work. You are looking for a pattern which is self-consistent and, if there are bits that don't fit in the pattern – the shop floor are miserable or the numbers don't add in or the product breaks, or whatever – you haven't got the right solution.'

Terence Stamp

The universe sent Terence to me down the airwaves. Memories came flooding back of standing in a lift with tears pouring down my face having just seen Billy Budd, *and finding myself staring, puzzled, into an identical pair of violet eyes. I remembered he was another unemployable on paper and he had just written* The Night, *which was apparently an extremely good novel! How had a so-called 'illiterate' become a wordsmith? I needed to find out.*

Terence engages his entire neurology in the discussion, so you never have to ask him where or how he experiences something because he demonstrates it while he is talking. His language is so precise about his internal processing, and his strategies for getting round his own objections to doing something are so ingenious, that I thought you would like to read his own account.

I went to school when I was three; and I just used to run away – it was like a nightmare. My mother felt that she would get arrested if I didn't go. They discovered I was playing hooky. I must have been quite smart! I used to get my mark and then, before the new teacher came in, I would slip out, and I was in the park all day, and got home at the right time – I was really little! My mother took me to the local doctor – the wise man of the community – who told her she didn't have to send me until I was five.

When I went two years later, I just couldn't learn anything: I couldn't learn to read; they tried to teach me how to knit and I was left-handed, so that made things much more complicated somehow; and I couldn't tie my shoes – I couldn't master anything.

Then there was this exam when I was eleven which was made to be so important by my family. There was all the emotional blackmail: I'd get a leather satchel, and maybe a bike. That was the first real hurdle that I had to take. I did not know how to prepare for it, because the learning-by-rote system just clamped my mind. Even when I learnt to read, it wasn't at school, it was because I wanted to read *Rupert Bear* – I was so mystified by the pictures that I thought there must be some secret in the writing; I had only just learnt to read when this exam came up.

To this day, I don't know how I managed to get through it.

The general knowledge paper had certain similarities to the one thing that I was kind of good at, with curious questions like, 'What does an E look like in the mirror?' (The school had changed from the one I went to when I was three: the old, frightening Gothic building was changed into a secondary school, and I went to another school, which was beautiful – so it was much less threatening.)

We were told about the scholarship and the headmaster said that, if we passed, we would go to a grammar school and, if we didn't, we would go to a secondary school – the same awful school that I had already been to! The Hammer Horror Film! And I knew it was filled with really rough kids, and I didn't want to go back there ever! Everything about it was frightening. The headmaster said, 'If you go to the grammar school you get a uniform and a cap … anybody who really wants to pass the scholarship: stand up'.

Nobody stood up. Nobody wanted to go. They were rough kids; they didn't want to go somewhere with a uniform, they wanted to be gangsters. I had this feeling that if I didn't stand up, I would fail; so I stood up, and I was the only one. The headmaster said, 'let's hope you're still standing after the scholarship'. I remember living in absolute torment for that school holidays, having to wait; and I remember when the letter arrived saying I had passed.

And there was an upturn, because I had all the trappings: a blazer; a cap; a satchel; a bike! I was put in 2D – the lowest class of the first year. I could see we were D – we weren't like A kids and B kids. They were sort of intellectuals and had spectacles. They studied things like languages, and we did things like woodwork. That first year I did learn, and I was getting 90 per cents. I thought to myself, 'I can go to Oxford University, I can row for Oxford; I had all these grandiose ideas!'

Then, in the second year I moved up to 3C (so I had moved up a grade) and, in that year, I realized it was just more lists, and that the lists were interminable. For French, there was a whole book of verbs – and all conjugated differently, and I just knew I couldn't do that! [Clamping his head with this hands]. I just closed down and they gave up on me as well.

If I had to tell you how I learned, how I matured, I would say 'heroes'. One boy called Roy was everything: incredibly good looking; the opening bat in the cricket team; good at football; sang like Dean Martin. He was a year older than me and I thought to myself, 'I will just watch him, because he's such a star, it's not going to be any problem for him – he's going to know the moves.' So I just stuck close to him like a mascot. I followed the table tennis team. I would watch how he did things, just to play like that: he had a grace that showed itself as a kind of effortlessness. It was wonderful to watch him do anything: you never saw him under duress. It was great! It was cool!

And then there was this terrible evening when somebody asked him what he was going to do, now that he was leaving school. He said his dad had apprenticed him at a printing company. My world collapsed; I couldn't believe that I had to make my own rope, that I had to make my own ladder.

At this time we'd got a TV, and I started saying that the things that I saw were not very good and that I could do it better. And my dad, who didn't talk much anyway, looked me in the eye and said, 'Listen, son. People like us don't do things like that. Look, son, I don't want you to talk about it any more.'

And I was changed from a boiling kettle to a pressure cooker. I was sixteen and I was now just building up a head of steam. I was too young to leave home, so I did what my parents wanted for two years. I went into advertising and I was earning a lot of money by the time I was eighteen. I had my own department and I used to make myself look older: make-up, glasses with ordinary lenses, because I was this kid!

But there was a sense of disappointment and dissatisfaction at having an ordinary job – I had good money, I had clothes, I was going out to dances but there was this profound sense of emptiness. I wasn't exposed to any heroes, I wasn't meeting the kind of people that I could admire, that I could identify with, that I could model myself on. It was sort of tawdry. It was like that feeling I had with the scholarship, 'If I don't do this, now, my whole life I'm going to regret it.'

I left home and started to go to evening drama classes. I had become a really great table tennis player, I had a trial for Essex and I was hanging out with the best young players in the world (*all this, from modelling Roy!*) But I had to sacrifice that and I had this very tough life here, living in penury. But I was becoming. And then I realized that the only way I would ever have any chance of becoming a fully-paid member of the industry would be to go to a drama school, and I would have to win a scholarship. When I confronted that, I had to confront everything I had hated about school. I had to learn the lines; I had to study Shakespeare – all the things that were totally beyond me at school. I hated it, but it was the price of the ticket.

I discovered a secret about learning: I realized that I had to be subversive with my mind. I said to myself, 'Today, we're only going to learn the first line and, if necessary, we are only going to learn half the first line.'

I would write down the first line on a bit of paper and I'd put it in my pocket; I'd walk around with the first line in my pocket and I'd take it out and look at it; and then, the next morning, I'd say to myself, 'Now, we're not going to learn the second line, until we know the first one,' and I'd get up and say the first line and, if I had any doubt at all, I would not allow myself to go on to the second. Of course, pretty soon, I was learning the lines in five minutes.

Today, the learning is an inner process, but the inner process of the learning is consciously going through fear. For me, it is in solving the inner problems that success is reflected outwardly. When I write, it is another feeling – it is what I think of as the right brain being active. I think that the problem of education is that it is only left brain oriented.

Where and when he learns

It's to do with the absence of threat. All my autobiographies were written while I was filming, the logic being: this time is paid for, so I can do this bit of scribbling and, if I get anything, it's a bonus – I am just using time spent waiting around. I write on the back of scripts, which takes away the threat of the white page. I have very soft pencils which write very easily – and they are round so as not to drag on my hand. I have incredibly soft rubbers.

Where and when he does not learn

You get into a space where you really cannot learn. I refuse to write articles and things because that is a deadline – it is not my kind of writing, it is not free. I'm aware that a lot of the time the car is driving down the road and the driver is asleep: these centres in my body are working inharmoniously and doing each other's jobs, which they are not equipped to do. They are in order when I have the light of my consciousness focused upon them [demonstrating that this comes from the front, left side of his head]. Sometimes I have to say, 'Wait a minute! I'm going to think what I want to think: you are meant to feel things, you're not going to use this thinking. This is for catching a train, it is not for imagining all kinds of tragedies and nonsense.' We are at the mercy of ourselves and most people won't accept that.

How he learns

When I am aware that I am present in the moment, that moment is often accompanied by a sensation of an expansion of space in the middle of my head. It's like the space in the middle of an apple: the apple is sealed, but if you cut it in half there is a space around the seeds. And if you cut open the seed, there's a space in the middle of the seed. It's a kind of non-sensation: I experience what's pushed out by the space. When I am there, I learn automatically: it's non-action, everything falls into that void, everything falls into that stillness – into that perfectly balanced mind.

If we look back over our lives, we can see moments of extraordinary clarity when we really remember things; we were there – but it was accidental, somehow. What we are talking about now is making conscious those things which had previously been accidental. If I can change myself, the world is different.

What he is doing on this planet

Remembering to be there; because it's only real when I am. Everything is subject to change, except the feeling that I am. I know that because I remember it when I was little; the first snow; or walking out onto a quiet, warm street – when I was there, and I knew I was there. It is a natural state. We were born into that state and I think that one of the purposes of life is to return to that consciously.

Who he is in relation to others

When you are there, and you know you are there, there is no separation. There isn't another. For there to be another, thought has to be talking, 'She's there; she's different; she's Diana ...' It's all thought talking but, once you notice that thought is moving, the noticing of it ends it.

Most people find that the moment they notice that they have not got any internal dialogue running, it starts up again. Terence does things the other way round, which is remarkably clever.

I don't mess with the mind because that is just thought, dealing with more thought. I just refocus my attention, 'what is the body feeling at the moment?'

On giving ourselves a hard time

We will give up anything but we won't give up the things that hurt us. We hold on; we allow them to torture us. We'll give up the good things: we'll fast and deprive ourselves, but we won't give up what hurts us. It's so obvious, but it's so hard to admit.

Judith DeLozier

Judy has been involved in NLP since the early 1970s, bringing her own work from different religions, anthropology and dance into the field. She trains all over the world, as well as at home with Robert Dilts and Todd Epstein at the NLP University. The influence of dance shows in everything she says and does.

Where and when she learns

I have this belief that there are masses of things to learn, just lurking everywhere. The question is, 'Am I noticing those things?' Or, 'Am I in a state or a place to notice those things?' I think I am always learning; although I may not know what it is I am learning. There are some places where maybe there is a tendency to make an assumption that I know something, and, over time, I have understood that that is the bigger challenge.

Where and when she does not learn

There is something about certain kinds of conflict where it makes it more difficult for me to learn – at least it did in the past. What I was putting in the muscle was the tension and the conflict, and that would get in the way of me being clear. It was wear and tear on my body; so I had to find a dance between where it is appropriate for me to put the information in the muscle, and where it is appropriate for me to see it just from the outside. It has to do with my belief about balance and about ecology for myself and what is going on around me.

When I go into another culture and I'm modelling for, say, relational patterns, they get marked a lot in the kinaesthetic system [indicating her heart], but not always. Or maybe they initially get marked there as 'Attend! Attend! There's something happening there and this is important: there's a pattern there'; and then there's a point at which the words will get louder and then they'll soften, or a picture will just brighten and then almost come forward and then recede; it's just marked out as, 'There's something here', and I may not know what it is yet.

Sometimes it gets marked just in the heart, sometimes it gets marked in all systems. I don't know whether that's just timing; maybe all of it does get marked here first. Maybe I notice it, maybe I don't. Maybe it happens several times, but once it gets 'woom! woom!' [demonstrating advancing/retreating information with her hands] then I know that there is something there that I can focus on.

I don't learn on the telephone; I know that is because I have this thing about being robbed of information.

Q. What else stops you from learning?
It could be time; it could be my interest in the content.

Q. How do you know when something is interesting?
There's a feeling in here; it's warm and something that touches my heart.

What she does and does not learn

The things that I am going to be drawn to as interesting and important for me are going to touch my heart. There is also the set of realities that go 'This may not touch your heart and it is something that is important to learn: it will make your life easier.' So it goes to that higher set of criteria which have to do with the overall balance. It is knowledge gained over time; and I can also see pictures of stressing out, running around Santa Cruz, trying to get taxes sorted out and so on, because I did not know certain, very simple things. And if I had learned those, it would make a lot of difference in how I felt. So again, it is wanting to maintain a certain balance; and for it to be easy. I like it to be easy; I am basically lazy.

How she learns

I put myself in situations where I have to come to my senses; where I can't go to sleep; where I have to be available. I make images of past experiences of what I think are similar situations and the way I responded in the past. I'm in the images, reliving them – at least partially; then I sort for differences. Then I start looking at those differences. I erase the context and try to let go of the presuppositions of labels and stuff. I try not to let that interfere. The thing about the labels is probably the biggest thing that I am aware of; and how I connect with other situations.

The more I fix my attention and filter in a certain way, the less systemic I become in my thinking. If you start thinking in a systemic fashion, the rest is a piece of cake and you begin to get a sense of when to fix your attention on something, when there's a rule in there, when there's a form in there.

How she does not learn

The process by which I don't learn is the opposite of the systemic stuff. I go, 'I don't know how these are connected', and if I can't find a way of connecting them and making a larger picture, knowing how it is going to connect to some other relevant factors in my life, then I just go into a trance. It's just straight priority of what I hold as valuable. So maybe I am not as curious. I am learning to be curious about money; I am learning to think of it as a game – and that's made a difference.

I told her that she really should learn to do her accounts. Her body stiffened and her head turned sharply away to the right.

I go, 'This is not part of my identity. It's not who I am. Waste my time on money? And little numbers? Where's the quality?' And now, what I am learning is that the quality is in the long term. This is the patience thing; I am not going to know how that is going to make a qualitative difference in my life in the short term. I am taking the words in because I have such a reflexive thing in me about separating the behaviour from the intent. The intention is that life be easy for me. I'm not aware of any pictures – there's more of a sense image about spending all this time sitting down and playing around with little numbers. It's not that it's bad, it's just like the ocean's out there! And the trees! And the people! Why would I want to focus on this?

Why she learns

Because it's wonderful! Because my map gets bigger and more of the world opens up. It's like recreating the world every day. It feels so darn good! It looks beautiful. It looks and sounds different every day. I believe we are built to continue to learn, and not to learn somehow is a sadness. If we are willing to continue to learn, if we are willing to really look at difference and appreciate it for difference, as opposed to thinking of it as a threat, it brings some hope into the world. And, of course, it's fun, which is one of my highest criteria for doing anything.

Q. 'Why do you believe all this?'
I think it's a useful way to be in the world. If I take the alternative, that it's not useful to learn, and start to set up filters so that information does not get in – that's sort of the living dead to me. Learning is exciting and fun and we're always doing it; it's more difficult to not do it.

Who?

That's always the hardest one for me. If I use the metaphor of the dancer, I think that I was a dancer before I was a dancer –

even though I was only learning to do a *plié* and a *tendu* and a *dégagé*, the quality with which I did each one of those little chunks was with the depth and the spirit of a dancer, even though I couldn't put them together yet. So that was an indication to me of deeper identity, and dancing in communication being a deeper sort of metaphor for who I am.

Who else?

In relation to your nearest and dearest?
The word that comes is 'gifts'. I am for them, and they are for me, a continually opening gift – a gift inside a gift, and another gift inside that gift. Sometimes it's hard to get the bow untied, and sometimes it's easy.

In relation to colleagues and friends?
Well, also, many of those people are gifts. There's a continual unfolding of more of this mind that has to do with the group mind, that none of us could do alone: it requires that relationship to unfold. Maybe that's also part of the gift in the larger sense.

In relation to the planet?
A little, tiny, tiny person, who has a tiny, tiny but very important mission that only I can do. Part of it is taking NLP to other parts of the world where it's not yet, but the mission is not embodied in the NLP, it is embodied in me. So it is how the NLP is embodied in me as a model – it's not in the NLP technology. I have a deep belief that there is not anything that I could teach a person that they don't already deeply know; and it's a question of creating a context where people start to realize where we have forgotten and what we have forgotten, how we have disconnected, and the importance of reconnecting. If I have a mission it is that I can serve as a model in some form and go, 'Here's this set of technologies and processes and procedures and concepts that can satisfy this mind called consciousness, because it likes things in a certain order and in

a certain sequence of steps'. That's really cool, but that's sort of the earned fish. It's really the unearned fish: people deserve respect by the very fact that they are alive – if I can maintain that, then that would be my mission.

In relation to the universe?
The metaphor that comes to my mind – I think it's from the Hasidic Jewish tradition – when somebody dies, an entire universe has been destroyed. There's that sense of universes within universes, connecting with universes and universes, which continues to create bigger and bigger universes.

* * *

Postscript

As you will have discovered, all my models learn with ease if the subject interests them, if they can see and make a connection to something that they already know, or something that will be useful to them in the future. None of them learns under stress, and some of them align their conscious and unconscious minds by referring to or addressing themselves as 'we' or 'us' in tricky situations.

They all make pictures and involve their feelings which is pretty amazing, when 'received' thought would have it that words are everything, that seeing things that aren't there is not done, and that feelings have no place as far as the intellect is concerned. Somehow, these people managed to escape what they 'ought to' do, and went on using their own wonderfully efficient strategies.

They move freely among the three perceptual positions, absorbing information from all of them at different logical levels, connecting to past and future. They allow themselves to learn by being aware of what comes when their conscious minds are distracted.

The are confident in the knowledge that they do not know everything and this confidence allows them to align themselves to the beliefs that they hold according to the information that they have – knowing that they can change their minds if they have made a mistake, because mistakes are just another way of learning.

If there is a particularly loathsome subject that you really do need to get your head around, and you still find yourself reacting to it like Colin with his tax return, or Judy with 'all those little numbers', the ultimate lazy learning strategy is simply to move it into the file where you keep things that you love doing, making the pictures the same size, shape, quality, distance away from you and so on, as the pictures of the things you like. Or you can just pretend that you like it: act 'as if' you do, and see what happens.

Alternatively, you can add a piece of ritual to your change. This is known in the trade as a 'Circle of Excellence'.

> Create a circle on the ground where you can imagine that you are having enormous fun, doing your favourite thing and information is pouring in through every sense and at every level. Step into this circle, take a deep breath (inspiration) and be aware of what you are seeing, hearing, feeling, tasting and smelling, and how you are experiencing the evidence from these five senses. When you are fully aware of what is going on, you can step out of the circle and create another one, in a different place, where you can imagine that other thing that you do not enjoy, and be aware of what is going on inside you in that circle.
>
> Then, leaving your beliefs about the subject and your 'not learning' experiences in the second circle, you can step out into a third, neutral, circle.
>
> The final step is to take the subject into the first circle where you see, hear, feel, taste and smell things in the way that you do when you are having fun; take a deep breath – from the top of your head, to the tip of your nose, to the tips of your fingers and the tips of your toes – and enjoy the changes that you experience.

You can use these techniques in any situation. For example, if you hate making speeches, if you have to have a difficult discussion with somebody, if you are putting off doing your accounts, sorting out your paperwork, tidying up the kitchen, making that telephone call ...

You now have the patterns that you need. You have the knowledge of how you function when you are learning and what you do to stop yourself from learning. You have choices about how you are going to react in a learning situation. You have discovered that life is much simpler than you thought now that you have taken charge of your brain. What you do with this information is up to you.

Enjoy your self!

A Message from Dr Richard Bandler

It was not until well after this book was finished that I had the good fortune to be entranced by the genius who created NLP, and I thought he might be a most useful addition to your collection of mentors.

Words like 'you can't' and 'impossible' do not have a tranquillizing effect upon Richard, especially when uttered by bureaucrats or people supposedly in authority. When he hears tales about this sort of conversation, he is rather inclined to don helmet and leathers and ride his Harley Davidson right into the office of the person responsible:

Bureaucrat: You can't park that here!
Richard: I just did.

So, if you ever find yourself frustrated, paralysed or enraged by having other people's idiotic limitations imposed upon you, just call up his headquarters (Earth Coincidence Control) in your head and Sir Richard, in his shining helmet, upon his glistening charger, will roar into the inner sanctum of whoever is trying to limit your creativity, and by the time he has finished with them, they will be relieved to agree with any sensible suggestion.

Richard has written this postscript especially for you:

Time is As bountiful
And As wide
As your unconscious
is long so
live And
learn
unconsciously
Now.

Bibliography

These books are fiction to expand your thinking.

Adams, James L: *The Care and Feeding of Ideas*, Penguin Books, UK, 1986.

Andreas, Steve and Connirae: *Change Your Mind – and Keep the Change*, Real People Press, USA, 1987.

Andreas, Steve and Connirae: *The Heart of the Mind*, Real People Press, USA, 1989.

Agostini, Franco: *Visual Games*, Guild Publishing, UK, 1986.

Bandler, Richard and Grinder, John: *The Structure of Magic I*, Science and Behaviour Books, USA, 1975.

Bandler, Richard and Grinder, John: *Frogs into Princes*, Real People Press USA, 1979; Eden Grove Editions, UK, 1990.

Bandler, Richard; Grinder, John and Satir, Virginia: *Changing with Families*, Science and Behaviour Books, USA, 1976.

Bandler, Richard: *Using your Brain – for a Change*, Real People Press, USA, 1985.

Bandler, Richard: *Time for a Change*, Meta Publications, USA, 1993.

*Bandler, Richard: *The Adventures of Anybody*, Meta Publications, USA, 1993.

*Bach, Richard: *A Gift of Wings*, Pan Books, UK, 1976.

*Bach, Richard: *Illusions*, Pan Books, UK, 1977.

*Bach, Richard: *Jonathan Livingston Seagull*, Pan Books.

*Bach, Richard: *A Bridge Across Forever*, Pan Books, UK, 1985.

*Bach, Richard: *One*, Pan Books, UK, 1988.

Barlow, Wilfred: *The Alexander Principle*, Arrow Books, UK, 1973.

Bateson, Gregory: *Steps to an Ecology of Mind*, Jason Aronson Inc, USA, 1972.

Bateson, Gregory: *Mind and Nature*, Bantam Books, USA, 1988.

Benjamin, Harry: *Better Sight without Glasses*, Thorsons, UK, 1929.

Berne, Eric: *Games People Play*, Penguin Books, UK, 1964.

Berthérat, Thérèse: *The Body Has its Reasons*, Cedar Books, USA, 1977.

Bly, Robert: *Iron John: A Book about Men*, Vintage Books, USA, 1992; Element Books, UK, 1993.

Burley-Allen, Madelyn: *Listening – the Forgotten Skill*, John Wiley, USA, 1982.

Buzan, Tony: *Use Your Memory*, BBC Publications, UK, 1986.

Buzan, Tony: *Make the Most of Your Mind*, Pan Books, UK, 1977.

Campbell, Don: *Introduction to the Musical Brain*, MMB, USA, 1984.

Campbell, Don: *The Roar of Silence*, Quest, USA, 1989.

Capra, Fritjof: *The Tao of Physics*, Flamingo, 1976.

Cameron-Bandler, Leslie and Lebeau, Michael: *The Emotional Hostage*, Real People Press, USA, 1986.

Carlzon, Jan: *Moments of Truth: New Strategies for Today's Customer-Driven Economy*, Harper & Row, 1989.

Cassidy, John and Rimbeaux, B.C.: *Juggling for the Complete Klutz*, Klutz Press, USA, 1988.

Castaneda, Carlos: *The Teachings of Don Juan*, Penguin Books, UK, 1970.

Castaneda, Carlos: *Tales of Power*, Penguin Books, UK, 1976.

Castaneda, Carlos: *The Eagle's Gift*, Penguin, UK, 1982.

Castaneda, Carlos: *The Second Ring of Power*, Penguin Books, UK, 1979.

Crowley, Richard and Mills, Joyce: *Cartoon Magic*, Magination, USA, 1989.

Crum, Thomas: *The Magic of Conflict*, Touchstone, UK, 1988.

DeLozier, Judith and Grinder, John: *Turtles All the Way Down*, Grinder DeLozier Associates, USA, 1987.

Dhority, Lynn: *Acquisition through Creative Teaching*, Centre for Continuing Development, USA, 1984.

Dilts, Robert B.: *Albert Einstein: Neuro-Linguistic Analysis of a Genius*, Dynamic Learning Center, USA, 1990.

Dilts, Robert B.: *Wolfgang Amadeus Mozart: Songs from the Spirit*, Dynamic Learning Center, USA, 1992.

Dilts, Robert B., Epstein, Todd, and Dilts, Robert W: *Tools for Dreamers*, Meta Publications, USA, 1991.

Edwards, Betty: *Drawing on the Right Side of the Brain*, Fontana Books, UK, 1979.

Edwards, Betty: *Drawing on the Artist Within*, Fontana Books, UK, 1986.

Eicher, James: *Making the Message Clear: Communicating for Business*, Grinder DeLozier Associates, USA, 1987.

Feldenkrais, Moshe: *Awareness through Movement*, Penguin Books, UK, 1980.

Fisher, Roger and Ury, William: *Getting to Yes*, Hutchinson Business, UK, 1981.

Fordham, Frieda: *An Introduction to Jung's Psychology*, Penguin Books, UK, 1953.

Fritz, Robert: *The Path of Least Resistance*, Stillpoint, USA, 1984.

Gallwey, Timothy W.: *The Inner Game of Tennis*, Pan Books, UK, 1975.

Gallwey, Timothy W.: *The Inner Game of Golf*, Pan Books, UK, 1981.

Gallwey, Timothy W. and Kriegel, Robert: *The Inner Game of Skiing*, Pan Books, UK, 1977.

Gardner, Martin: *The Mathematical Magic Show*, Penguin Books, UK, 1985.

Gattegno, Caleb: *The Common Sense of Teaching Mathematics*, Educational Solutions, UK, 1974

Gilligan, Stephen G.: *Therapeutic Trances*, Brunner/Mazel, USA, 1987.

Gonzalez, Luis Jorge: *Excelencia Personal: Valores*, Editorial Font, Mexico, 1991.

Green, Barry with Gallwey, Timothy W.: *The Inner Game of Music*, Pan Books, UK, 1986.

Grinder, John and Bandler, Richard: *Trance-formations*, Real People Press, USA, 1981.

Grinder, Michael: *The Educational Conveyor Belt*, Metamorphous Press, USA, 1989.

Hart, Mickey: *Drumming at the Edge of Magic*, Harper, USA, 1990.

Harvey-Jones, John: *Making It Happen*, Collins, UK, 1988.

Harvey-Jones, John: *Managing to Survive*, Heinemann, UK, 1993.

Harvey-Jones, John: *Getting It Together*, Heinemann, UK, 1991.

Harvey-Jones, John: *Troubleshooter I*, BBC, 1990.

Harvey-Jones, John: *Troubleshooter II*, BBC, 1992.

Holt, John: *How Children Learn*, Pelican Books, UK, 1967.

Holt, John: *How Children Fail*, Penguin Books, UK, 1990.

Hudson, Liam: *Contrary Imaginations*, Pelican Books, UK, 1966.

Karbo, Joe: *The Lazy Man's Way to Riches*, Success Classics, USA, 1986.

Kline, Peter: *The Everyday Genius*, Great Ocean, USA, 1988.

Laborde, Genie: *Fine Tune Your Brain*, Syntony, USA, 1988.

la Garanderie, Antoine de: *Tous les Enfants peuvent reussir*, Editions du Centurion, France, 1988.

Lakoff, Georg and Johnson, Mark: *Metaphors We Live By*, University of Chicago Press, USA, 1980.

Leonard, George: *The Silent Pulse*, Dutton, USA, 1978.

Lewis, David: *The Alpha Plan*, Methuen, UK, 1986.

Lewis, David: *Mind Skills*, Souvenir Press, UK, 1987.

Living Values Parent Groups: A Facilitator Guide
Living Values Activities for Children Ages 3–7
Living Values Activities for Children Ages 8–14
Living Values Activities for Young Adults
(These four books are available from www.hci-online.com or from BKIS, 65 Pound Lane, London, NW10 2HH (020-8727-3389)

Lovelock, J. E.: *Gaia – A New Look at Life on Earth*, OUP, UK, 1979.

*Lynn, Jonathan and Jay, Anthony: *Yes Prime Minister*, BBC Publications, UK, 1986.

McMaster, Michael and Grinder, John: *Precision: A New Approach to Communication*, Precision Models, USA, 1980.

Meister Vitale, Barbara: *Unicorns are Real*, Warner, USA, 1982.

Meister Vitale, Barbara: *Free Flight*, Valmar, USA, 1986.

Moore, Robert and Gilette, Douglas: *King, Warrior, Magician, Lover*, Harper, USA, 1990.

Morris, Desmond: *Manwatching*, Triad Panther, UK, 1978.

O'Connor, Joseph: *Not Pulling Strings*, Lambent Books, 1987.

O'Connor, Joseph and Seymour, John: *An Introduction to Neuro-Linguistic Programming*, rev. edn, Aquarian Press, 1993.

Palmer, Adam: *Champneys Cookbook*, Boxtree, UK, 1993.

*Paulus, Trina: *Hope for the Flowers*, Paulist Press, USA, 1972.

Rhodes, Jerry and Thame, Sue: *The Colours of Your Mind*, Fontana Books, UK, 1988.

Rogers, Carl: *A Way of Being*, Houghton Mifflin Company, USA, 1980.

Rogers, Carl: *Dialogues*, Constable, UK, 1990.

Russell, Peter: *The Brain Book*, Routledge, UK, 1979.

Russell, Peter: *The Awakening Earth*, Fontana Books, UK, 1982.

*Saint-Exupery, Antoine de: *Le Petit Prince*, Gallimard, France, 1946.

Sams, Jamie and Carson, David: *Medicine Cards*, Bear & Co, USA, 1988.

*Satir, Virginia: *Self Esteem*, Celestial Arts, USA, 1975.

*Satir, Virginia: *Meditations and Inspirations*, Celestial Arts, USA, 1985.

Senge, Peter: *The Fifth Discipline: the Art and Practice of the Learning Organization*, Doubleday, UK, 1990.

Shone, Ronald: *Creative Visualisation*, Thorsons, UK, 1984.

*Stamp, Terence: *The Night*, Phoenix House, UK, 1993.

*Süskind, Patrick: *Perfume*, Penguin Books, UK, 1987.

Suzuki, Shinichi: *Nurtured by Love*, Ability Development, USA, 1983.

Valentine, Tom and Carole: *Applied Kinesiology*, Thorsons, UK, 1985.

van Nagel, etc: *Megateaching and Learning*, Southern Institute Press, USA, 1985.

Wanless, Mary: *Ride with Your Mind*, Methuen, UK, 1987.

Whitmore, John: *Superdriver*, RAC, UK, 1988.

Zukov, Gary: *The Dancing Wu Li Masters*, Flamingo, UK, 1982.

Some Useful Addresses

The Anglo-American Book Company Ltd
Crown Buildings
Bancyfelin
Carmarthen SA33 5ND
Tel: 01267 211880
Fax: 01267 211886
Email: books@anglo-american.co.uk
Website: www.anglo-american.co.uk

The Association of Neuro-Linguistic Programming
PO Box 5
Haverfordwest SA63 6YA
Contact: Caroline Coughlan
Email: admin@anlp.org
Website: http://anlp.org

Diana Beaver
c/o The Useful Book Company
The Cottage
Temple Guiting
nr Cheltenham
Gloucestershire GL54 5RP
Tel: 01451 850863
Fax: 01451 850455
Email: dianabeave@aol.com
Website: http://www.dianabeaver.co.uk

Living Values: An Educational Program Inc.
866 UN Plaza, Suite 436
New York 10017
Website: http://www.livingvalues.net

Living Values: An Educational Programme
3 Fullamoor Cottages
Clifton Hampden
Abingdon
Oxfordshire OX14 3DD
Contact: Lynn Henshall
Tel/Fax: 01865 408124
Email: britishisles@livingvalues.net
Website: http://www.livingvalues.net

McKenna Breen Ltd (Richard Bandler in the UK)
Aberdeen Studios
22–24 Highbury Road
London N5 2EA
Contacts: Michele Cornell and Shelley Loughney
Tel: 020 7704 6604
Fax: 020 7704 1679
Website: http://www.mckenna-breen.com

The NLP University (Robert Dilts and Judith Delozier)
The Dynamic Learning Center
PO Box 1112
Ben Lomond
California 95005
Contact: Teresa Epstein
Tel: 408 336 3457
Fax: 408 336 5854
Email: teresanlp@aol.com
Website: rdilts@ nlpu.com

The Society of Neuro-Linguistic Programming™
(Richard Bandler in the US)
268 Bush Street, Suite 4115
San Francisco
California 94014
Contact: Brahm von Huene
Tel: 415 882 4657
Fax: 415 974 0349
Email: 1st_inst@NLP-DHE.com
Website: www.NLP.DHE.com

Index

Acknowledgement 23, 25, 91, 76, 107, 165
Appleby, Sir Humphrey 26, 132–3
Attention, placing 5, 9, 78, 80, 175, 178
Auditory mode 9–11, 36, 61, 80–1, 85, 87–9, 107, 136
  skills, enhancing 68–76

Babies 10, 15, 21, 62, 71, 83, 84, 126
Bandler, Dr Richard xii, 184
Baroque music 70, 75
Bateson, Gregory 49–50, 79, 129, 132
Bees 16
Behaviour 4, 6, 17, 23, 25–6, 42, 50–2, 53, 84, 99, 102, 103, 107, 108–11, 123, 131, 133, 179
Beliefs 1, 4, 5, 6–9, 21, 24, 35, 40–7, 51, 102–4, 107, 110, 133, 136, 140, 168, 182
Blame 19, 22, 44, 56, 102, 126, 139, 166
Blindfolded, exercises 10, 78–9, 140
Boundaries of self 79–80
Brain cells 16, 45
Brain waves 15, 18
Brains, left and right 14, 32–3, 132, 173

Brains, our three 12–16
  left/right 14, 18, 32–3, 173
Breathing 80–81

Cadre Noir 128
Campbell, Don 69, 71, 125
Capabilities 35, 50, 51, 102, 110, 136
Castaneda, Carlos 107
Cause and effect programs 12
Change, fear of 47, 51, 52–4
Chant 71
Chemistry 35, 84, 110
Children 3, 7, 10, 15, 19–27, 34, 38, 42–4, 47, 52–4, 58, 64, 84, 102–3, 118, 120, 126–7, 161
Christmas tree 57
Classroom experiences 22, 30, 31, 34, 40–45
Coding 2, 60, 69, 120, 145
Communication 2, 4, 5, 24, 43, 69, 84, 91, 103, 122–3, 151, 155–6, 165, 167–9, 180
Confidence 56–7, 94, 144, 147, 150, 152, 155–7, 159, 181–2
Conscious/unconscious 16–18, 24, 28, 32–4, 39–41, 67, 72, 122, 181
Cooking 3, 84, 110, 145, 146, 147
Creativity 3, 15, 45, 98, 120, 184
Criticism 22–3, 102–4
Cross-referencing 11, 60

Cube, the Necker 7, 62
Cuisenaire Rods 41, 120
Curiosity 6, 44–5, 99, 111, 127,
    131, 134

DeLozier, Judith 5, 74, 78, 81,
    125, 129, 135, 176–81, 182
Depression 71, 78
Dialogue, internal 4, 8, 37, 46, 71–2,
    76, 86, 89, 94, 97, 119, 158
Dictation 118–19
Difference xiii, 5, 74, 119, 136,
    164, 178, 179
Dilts, Robert 23, 40, 49, 98, 110,
    120, 125, 129, 132, 136, 176
Displacement activity 38, 97
Dolphins 14, 132
Dream beyond the dream 58–9
Dyslexia 44, 51, 116, 119

Education 3, 20, 69, 118, 124,
    166, 173
Edwards, David 135, 137–41
Einstein, Albert 36, 106, 120, 124,
    130
Elders and betters, our 7, 26, 47,
    51, 89, 126–7
Emotions 12, 14, 27, 72, 169
Epstein, Todd 23, 40, 49, 98, 107,
    110, 129, 132, 136, 176
Evidence procedures 41, 94–6,
    107, 169
Excellence xiii, 164, 182
Eye movements 11, 64–9, 72–3, 78

Failure 24, 41, 46, 51, 64, 71, 97,
    102, 139, 142, 155, 160,
    166, 167, 171
Falconry 103, 107
Families 5–6, 21–4, 26, 27, 28, 35,
    44, 52–3, 54–5, 58, 96, 122,
    170
Fear 23, 38, 59, 127, 154, 173
Feedback 97, 158
Feet, position of 81

Filing systems 2, 8, 9, 11, 20, 64,
    69, 73, 78, 182
Filter systems 35, 62, 68, 95, 117,
    178, 179
Fish metaphors 131–2, 134, 181
Flexibility 36, 55, 89, 127, 128, 129
Foreign languages 4, 36, 122–3,
    171
Foveal vision 86

Gallwey, Timothy 17, 76–7, 125
Gattegno, Caleb 120
Gaze hounds 87
Generalizing 160
Geometry 6, 121–2
Goals 87, 114 *see also* outcomes
Golf 125, 141, 143, 162
Green, Lucinda 130, 135, 151–7
Grinder, John xii, 25, 42, 58, 59,
    62, 79, 81, 125, 129

Harman, Catherine 135, 141–4
Harmony 49, 70, 71, 75, 136, 157
Harvey-Jones, Sir John 1, 135,
    164–9
Heroes 167, 172
Hobbies 6, 27, 111–12
Holt, John 43
Honesty 137, 139, 140
Hypnosis 60

Identity 8, 47, 50–1, 53, 84,
    102–4, 107, 110, 119, 123,
    131, 165, 179, 180
Imagination 3, 49, 68, 82, 85, 115,
    116, 120, 150, 154
Inadequacy 1, 2, 26, 127, 132,
    157, 166, 167
Individuality 3–4, 23, 27, 36, 41,
    86, 104, 121, 167
Intention, positive 17, 26, 39, 96, 179
Interrupting 21, 72
IQ tests 37, 42
Juan, Don 107
Judging 26, 119

Juggling 72, 125
Jungle Gym 110, 111, 136

Kinaesthetic mode 10–11, 61, 74,
    79, 80–1, 87–9, 107
  skills, enhancing 76–82

Labelling 2, 119, 178
Language patterns xii, 11, 65–6,
    85, 136
Languages, foreign 4–5, 36, 52,
    72, 122–3, 124, 171
Learn, how we do 9–19
  how we do not 37–40
  what we do 6–9
  what we do not 40–7
  when/where we do 27–9
  when/where we do not 30, 35
  why we do 6–9
  why we do not 40–7
Learning through our bodies
    76–82
  ears 69–71
  eyes 61–8
  taste and smell 83–5
Lewis, Dr David 15, 37–8, 43, 45,
    62, 125
Lies, telling 3, 45
Listening 21, 28, 49, 70, 71–4, 81,
    85, 105, 119, 139, 141,
    143–4, 156, 160–1, 165, 168
Living Values 55
Logical levels of thinking 50–1,
    102–4, 105, 110–11, 123,
    131, 136, 181

Manners 44, 127
Marriage, evidence procedures in
    96
Matching/mirroring 6, 107–8, 165
Maths 6, 24, 35, 41, 52, 70, 106,
    120–2, 138, 152
McDermott, Ian 22, 101, 106, 128
McWhirter, John 86
Memory, auditory 69, 73–4

filing system for 115–17
  kinaesthetic 82
  photographic 46, 118
  visual 14, 64–8
Mentors 52, 128–30, 161, 184
Meta mirror 98–101, 110
Metaphor 51–2, 122, 131–4
Micro-muscle movement 16, 82
Mind reading 22
Mirroring 107 *see also* matching
Mistakes 7, 9, 17, 21, 26, 28, 74,
    117, 119, 126, 136, 143, 182
Modal operators 35
Modelling 4–5, 10, 23–4, 26, 50,
    52, 77, 80–2, 89, 107, 119,
    122–3, 130, 135–6, 172–3,
    177
Music 3, 12, 69–70, 72–3, 77

Necker cube 7, 62
Neurology xii, 11, 21, 27, 98, 112,
    160, 168, 170
NLP x–xi, 4, 5, 12, 17, 20, 22, 23,
    50, 84, 86, 97, 133, 135,
    158, 176, 180, 184

O'Connor, Joseph 12, 78, 125
Okayness 28
Other people, effects of and on 1,
    4, 6, 21, 31, 42, 53–5, 98,
    107–8, 111
Outcomes 24, 56–7, 59, 89, 94,
    103, 104, 160 *see also* goals

Palmer, Adam 135, 144–50
Perception 62, 151, 169
Perceptual positions 110, 181
Peripheral vision 86, 94, 108
Phobias 162
Photographic memory 46, 64–8,
    89, 118
Physiology 5, 77, 99, 118–19, 123,
    165
Pictures, internal 2, 4, 8–9, 14,
    31, 37, 41, 46, 65–7, 72, 76,

94–5, 114, 119, 143, 153–4, 156, 169

Polarity responders 35

Positions, perceptual 98–101, 110, 136, 181

Pressure 15, 33–4, 45, 145, 149, 150 *see also* stress

Presuppositions 43, 178

Pretending 40, 45–6, 76, 123, 182

Pritchard, James 131

Problem solving 108–11

Processing of information 4, 14, 24, 67, 90, 114, 120, 124, 145, 158, 170, 178

Programming xii–xiii, 9, 22, 24, 26, 71, 104, 166, 167

Protection, self 8, 17, 18, 22, 25–6, 39–40, 84, 86, 124, 126, 127, 130, 133–4, 161

Questions, asking 33, 43–5, 51, 53, 102–3, 104–7, 127, 130

Rapport 107, 148, 162, 165

Reading 20, 35, 114–17, 119, 170

Reality 2, 7, 45, 77, 121, 139, 169

Reeve, Colin 80, 135, 158–63, 182

Relationships 1, 19, 28, 50, 53, 88–9, 99, 132, 136, 166, 180

Relaxation 75–6, 90–3

Representations of reality 2, 9–11

Rhythm 5, 39, 69, 70–3, 78, 80, 82, 165

Right/left 32

Right/wrong 2, 22–3, 26, 32, 45, 53, 74, 139–40

Saliva 37, 84, 92

School 26, 30–1, 34–5, 52–3, 102, 105, 119, 139, 147, 149, 151–2, 166, 170–3

Science 35, 121, 124, 125

Self 17–18, 57–8, 79–80, 132, 162

Senses 2, 9–11, 39, 60–93, 140, 145, 178, 182

Should/ought to/must 35

Slime mould 124

Software 24–5, 45, 144

Sompa, Titos 71, 81

Sound 39, 68–74, 125

Spelling 9, 35, 82, 117–18

Stamp, Terence 135, 169–74

Strategies 2, 4, 7, 24, 27, 28, 39, 41, 60, 66, 67, 74, 102, 135, 149, 165, 169, 170, 181, 182

Stress 9, 25, 33–4, 37, 38, 39, 110, 181 *see also* pressure

Subjective experience xii, 50, 165

Success 24, 25, 47, 49, 52, 59, 94, 97, 119, 135, 139, 148, 155, 161, 167, 173

Survival 2, 12, 14, 21, 85, 122, 124, 127

Suzuki, Professor Shinichi 20, 23

Task/relationship 87–9, 132, 136

Time, thinking about 114–27, 136

Timelines 112, 114–17

Tomatis, Professor Alfred 70–1

Treasure hunting 111–14

Values 50, 55, 133, 140, 165

Vinci, Leonardo da 125, 130

Violin 20

Visual mode 9–11, 61, 69, 80–1, 85, 87–8, 107, 122, 124, 136, 156, 169

skills, enhancing 61–8

Vulnerability 84, 99, 126

Watching 21, 63, 64, 76, 99, 103, 142–3, 151, 153, 165

Whitmore, Sir John 17, 77, 125

Winning 15, 18, 141–2, 173

Writing 35, 114–19, 147, 170, 174

Zero 121